P9-AOY-702

THE OCEANA LIBRARY ON THE UNITED NATIONS

Study Guide Series
on the
United Nations
and
Related Agencies

FOR PEACE
AND THE
DIGNITY OF MAN

This book — fifth of a Series of Study Guides about the United Nations and related inter-governmental agencies designed especially for use in libraries and by teachers, group leaders, and students — is published by Oceana Publications, Inc. The material was assembled by the UNESCO Youth Institute, under the auspices of UNESCO and in co-operation with the United Nations and the other organizations covered in the series.

Acknowledgments are extended to the contributors in the inter-governmental agencies and to Dr. R. William Jones and his UNESCO Youth Institute staff.

United Nations Educational, Scientific, and Cultural Organization. Youth Institute.

1964
Oceana Publications, Inc.
Dobbs Ferry, N. Y.

Study guide series on the United Nations and related agencies.

6/67 = v.34,

Contents

Part I

Human Rights—The Dignity of Man

Part II

The United Nations—Who Needs It?

Appendices

Part I

HUMAN RIGHTS —
THE DIGNITY OF MAN

CHAPTER I

What Do We Mean By Human Rights?

What is a man worth?

Can the answer be given in dollars, or pounds, or francs, or roubles?

No! For no one can measure how much another individual values *himself*.

Of course, a man can give away his own life for some ideal or purpose outside himself, which he decides is "worth" more than he is. Or he can give up things that he needs for himself—food, or education, or freedom to do what he wants—for the service of others. In daily life, he often does so of his own volition. But for somebody else to deprive him of these things is to deprive him of his "rights."

What does he ask of his neighbors and fellow citizens? He asks that they respect his life, that is to say his existence on this earth, his basic physical needs as a human being, his earthly possession, his peace of mind, and such like. In return, he realizes that he must respect theirs. For this is the only way in which society can live together.

This is what we mean when we say that man is a *social* animal. One man's right is another man's obligation. There are duties which he owes to his fellow men, and duties which he expects his fellow men to have towards him. Because he is a human being, he has human rights which he shares with all his fellows.

On that account, "Human Rights" cannot be discussed merely as an abstract matter, as a philosophical concept, but only as the day-to-day experience of men and women everywhere. For example, if a person is shut out from his own country or finds himself unable to get employment because of the color of his skin, or is imprisoned or put to torture because of what he be-

1

lieves—in every such case his human rights are being infringed. Actual cases like these are happening every day. That is why the subject of human rights is a very live and immediate one and effects everybody.

WHY DECLARATIONS ARE MADE

Because human rights are a social problem, men have had to club together to obtain their recognition and enjoyment. It is natural that human rights should develop as society develops. Thus, from time to time, "declarations" of their rights are made by certain groups when they have found themselves down-trodden or badly treated by other men or by the rulers of the society in which they live. So it will be useful, at the beginning of this pamphlet, to glance back at the history of how human rights have appeared to previous generations and what men have done to defend or advance them. The next chapter, then, will review the main stages by which recognition of these rights has grown and been upheld.

Since human rights have meaning only in a social context, one of the first things we notice is that they bring us into the field of law. Law is the means by which individuals are related together in any given community and by which they enjoy, or should enjoy, the best things of life together.[1] And law has a great deal to do with what we call freedom — the freedom of the individual to live his life as he wants to, provided this freedom of his does not make it difficult or impossible for his fellow men to live the same way. Law, therefore, is the foundation of human rights and, particularly, of those individual freedoms which may be considered as basic to all other human rights.

Until recent times, the law affecting human rights has been *national* law. But, as this pamphlet seeks to explain, the time has come when the question of guaranteeing or enlarging the scope of human rights has overflowed the boundaries of the nation-state and become recognised as a world problem. So it has become more and more the subject of *international* law.

THE PROTECTION OF FREEDOM IS A CHIEF CONCERN OF LAW

Sometimes the process is a very complicated and difficult one.

---

[1] The Study Guide Series, Volume I, in this series, goes further into this matter. See Part II, "The Rule of Law."

2

It is this relationship between law and freedom which will become clearer as examples are given of different kinds of rights and how much time and energy has been expended on achieving or maintaining them.

That brings us, in turn, into the realm of government. For government is to a great extent the instrument of law in any given society. To some extent, in all states, it makes the law. The following chapters will trace some of the ways by which national governments have upheld human rights by enacting and implementing good laws—or otherwise.

In addition to the continuing efforts of most governments to progress in their own laws for the protection of human rights, these rights have increasingly become a world problem and have become part of a new system of *international* protection which is still in its early stages. It is at this point that we move, in the next chapter, into the field of the United Nations and its famous Universal Declaration of Human Rights.

AREAS OF HUMAN NEED

In subsequent chapters, the subject will divide into several different areas of human need and experience. In taking up some of the key points for more detailed explanation, we shall have to relate them to the various commissions or other UN bodies, which are frequently referred to in the daily press. This new international machinery has helped to define and strengthen different kinds of human rights and millions of unhappy people have been enormously benefitted. For example, there are the special rights of women and of children, of refugees and stateless persons, of workers in their jobs, and of religious and other particular groups. The most important of these find some place under the general headings of the Universal Declaration, which form the framework of the following pages.

At the end of each chapter there appears a short series of questions or problems, for further investigation by the reader or for discussion by the study group or seminar. At the end of the pamphlet will be found a suggested reading list carrying the topics further.

Since it will not be necessary to repeat word for word the whole text of the Universal Declaration in the following chapters, the complete text of the Declaration is printed separately as an Appendix for ready reference.

DISCUSSION SUGGESTIONS

1. "The rights of the individual do not spring from the fact that he is the citizen of a given state, but from the fact that he is a member of the human family." Is this statement true? Discuss the place of state laws in ensuring the enjoyment of the rights of its citizens. Are such laws sufficient? If not, why not?

2. Before reading this pamphlet further, make out a rough list of the rights you yourself consider essential for every human being to enjoy. Then compare your list with a quick glance over the Declaration. How far does *your* list reflect your own environment or experience? What rights do you notice in the Declaration which especially surprise you?

CHAPTER II

How Did Human Rights Get Into The Charter?

Looking back, it would seem that man's "progress" has been at the mercy of two opposing forces. One the one hand, successive generations have suffered the terrors and unspeakable brutalities of "man's inhumanity to man," expressed in recurrent wars and persecutions and pogroms. Far from lessening, it might seem that the 20th century has made no advance on man's barbaric past. The racial fanaticisms of the Nazis and Fascists, the horrors of the concentration camps, which culminated in the destruction of millions of human beings by the time the Second World War had ended, seem to have become almost a set pattern of our so-called "civilization."

Can it not, in fact, be claimed that the contempt for human values, displayed in such recent experiences as these, has led up to the unstable situation in the world today, which has often been summed up—militarily speaking—as the "Balance of Terror"? It is not surprising, therefore, that in this tragic context, the protection of human rights has turned out to be an extremely difficult and, often, slow and disappointing procedure.

A GREEK ANALOGY

Yet, on the other side of the picture, we have to recognize that, over the centuries, there has been evidenced an ever-increasing effort to spread peace and goodwill among men, both within one's local community and between different communities. There would seem to be a good deal of truth in the analogy drawn by a Greek poet, who pictured the progress of mankind as that of an eagle chained by the collar to a dog. If you feed the dog, the eagle is dragged into the dust; but if you feed the eagle, runs the poet's imagination, the eagle soars with the dog into the skies! It is in studying the actual plans and methods involved that we can draw hope and encouragement from the progress that man has actually made in so many fields of international co-operation. This series of Study Guides bears ample testimony to man's constant reaching out for better things —not least in the growth of human rights.

For example, spiritual leaders at different epochs have shown that the great religions they have founded or developed—Christianity, Buddhism, Judaism, Confucianism, and Mohammedanism —have all contained within them, and have tried to express, the basic idea of man's individual quality and also his need, or "right," to live the good life. In the long run, these great religions have tended towards the strengthening of co-operation between men. They have strengthened the mutual respect of man for man, even if, at times, religious fanatics have used their own beliefs as a means of conflict between the different groups. At least, all the main religions of earlier centuries did result in proclaiming man's rights as an *individual*. They brought these beliefs into conscious discussion, so that, later on, they became the basis of political, civic, cultural and other rights in their turn.

Slowly, in legal codes and the books of learned authors, human rights began to be defined. Then, public "declarations" began to be made of what man's rights should be—for example, that all men should be treated as equal in the eyes of the national law. Such "declarations" have played a vital role in setting down these rights for rulers to observe and for future generations to practice.

THE MAGNA CARTA

One of the first of these was the Magna Carta in England in 1215.[1] Although the rights—"privileges," they were called—set down in this charter or declaration were confined to a special class of land-owning barons at that time, the basic principles

---

[1] The Magna Carta begins: "The GREAT CHARTER of the LIBERTIES OF ENGLAND"; and it gave "to all the freemen of Our Realm these liberties underwritten, to have and to hold to them and their heirs, of Us and Our Heirs for ever." The twenty-ninth chapter continues: "No freeman shall be taken, or imprisoned, or be disseised of his freehold, or liberties . . . nor will we condemn him, but by the lawful judgment of his peers . . . We will sell to no man, we will not deny or delay to any man, either justice or right."

of the Magna Carta were gradually applied to an ever-widening group of the population. Eventually they became the acknowledged rights of all Englishmen. But, unless they had been so plainly recorded in this public way and solemnly agreed upon by the "powers that be," it is doubtful whether they would have attained the influence they had in later history.

A BILL OF RIGHTS

In 17th century England, a Bill of Rights was one of the several documents drawn up and presented in 1689 by the Commons to the King, as a statement of principles which the King's Government had to acknowledge as legally binding on them and as a guide to the ruling of the country. This idea of a "bill" of rights has been, as we know, extended in later centuries to other countries.

As time went on, the definition of a given people's rights became more precise and detailed. For example, in 1776, the historic Declaration of Independence set down the political and civic rights of the New World which, across the Atlantic, had emerged from the thirteen English colonies. The rights set forth in the Declaration were, a few years later, included in the American Constitution. In other words, a new system of government was built on the foundation of the human rights declared in this way. When we come to study the terms of the Universal Declaration of Human Rights we shall be struck by the similarity of some of the ideas contained in it to the national efforts which preceded them.

A few years later, in 1789, the declaration of "The Rights of Man" became the popular motivation of the French Revolution. Here was a standard below which the people felt their government should never fall. It listed in simple language the rights which, during the following century, became gradually accepted in nearly all countries as the basis of Western political life. Even authoritarian or highly-centralized states, which are frequently accused of denying freedom to the individual, generally include these basic "Rights of Man" in their state constitutions. Rights asserted by one group of citizens in one country have always tended to spread abroad and, sooner or later, have been acknowledged in other parts of the world as *universal* rights.

7

HUMANITARIANISM ARRIVES

The 19th century became known as the Century of Humanitarianism. (The eagle began to be fed, in preference to the dog.) Many reformist movements developed in the industrialized countries, aimed at bettering the daily life and improving the conditions of the new class of workers in mines and factories, which had been produced by the mechanisation of the production known as the Industrial Revolution. The new industrial worker was often described by the significant term "hand". "HANDS WANTED"—frequently ran an employer's appeal for workers. Human beings were being regarded as merely subsidiary to the machines they worked.

So, alongside individual rights, the concept of civil or political rights, and economic or social rights, began to gain public attention. National movements—such as trade unions—were formed, which greatly strengthened these rights and compelled governments to enforce them by enacting new laws. Some of these laws were called "emancipation" laws, as when slavery was legally abolished, or Jews or Catholics were allowed to worship as they pleased or to own landed property; and others were called "franchise" laws, as when women or non-property owners were allowed to vote in elections.

It was during the 19th century, too, that international organizations of all kinds began to form. They not only advanced the world's scientific and economic life enormously, but they began to improve the lot of ordinary citizens generally, promoting better health, education, travel, and cultural life. Such organizations as these eventually became the World Meteorological Organization, the Universal Postal Union, and other technical bodies which are now called the Specialized Agencies of the UN.

One thing which became increasingly apparent from this development in community growth was the fact that the individual's "rights" were inseparably linked with the degree of political, economic and social progress they enjoyed—one good reason, as we shall see, why the main topics of this pamphlet come within the ambit of the UN Economic and Social Council today. Simply put: What is the use of giving a man the right to vote, if he is starving? All human rights—personal, political, economic, social, religious—belong together and depend on each other.

WAR, THE UNIVERSAL ENEMY

Yet—alas!—all this steady trend towards world unity and humanitarian co-operation broke down almost completely with the outbreak of the First World War. Global conflict began in 1914 in Europe and, following an unstable 20-year period of "armistice," lasting from 1919 until 1939, broke out again as the Second World War. When it ended in 1945, many parts of the earth were physically shattered and morally ruined. Whole countries were in a state of political and economic collapse or had disappeared as independent entities. New regimes and authoritarian systems were everywhere arising from the chaos of defeat and destruction and despair. It is against this dark background that the modern revival of human rights must be set.

But, in spite of this continuing human tragedy, the interwar years of 1919-39 had seen the birth and establishment of the League of Nations, based upon a Covenant and enjoying an eventual membership of over 50 sovereign states. The Covenant made it plain that the League was intimately concerned with human rights on many levels, such as the rights of refugees and stateless persons, political, cultural, or religious minorities, and the racially persecuted. On the basis of the principles laid down in the Covenant and developed by various organs and other bodies of the League, millions of refugees and stateless persons were helped to a better life and certain minority groups came off much better than would have been possible, if their fate had been left entirely to the devices of the nations which harboured them.

Yet such efforts were small in comparison with what has been achieved under the United Nations Charter since the Second World War. The beneficient work of the 1919-39 period was brought almost to an end, as noted above, with the outbreak of the hideous persecution and political intolerance which led up to and culminated in the mass atrocities of the Second World War.

Was this, then, to be the end of the Rights of Man? Did it mean that so long and checkered a history had finally succumbed to the brute in man? Was there so little progress left to show for all the valiant struggles of the centuries?

It is important, therefore, to recall how the torch of human freedom was kept alight during the surrounding darkness of war and rekindled for the years of the new peace. It was, in fact, during the midst of the conflict that President Roosevelt issued in 1941 a statement proclaiming "The Four Freedoms"—namely, freedom of speech, freedom of religion, freedom from want, and freedom from fear. This philosophy of hope was put forward as a rallying cry of the Allied effort and became the basis of the "peace aims" to be attained at the end of the conflict.

Soon after this, steps were taken by the United Kingdom and the United States jointly to formulate such peace aims in more detail. This led to the publication of the Atlantic Charter which, among other things, laid down assurances "that all the men in all the lands may live out their lives in freedom from fear and want."

Before the slaughter had come to an end, plans were put in hand for the convening of an international conference to do for the post-war world what the League of Nations had attempted to do, but failed, before the Second World War. Thus it came about that at San Francisco, on 26 June 1945, fifty nations unanimously adopted the Charter of the United Nations which laid down the principles and working machinery of a new world order, wherein "We the Peoples" proclaimed our determination henceforth "to practice tolerance and live together in peace with one another as good neighbours."

HUMAN RIGHTS IN THE UN CHARTER

Among the Charter's fundamental principles are those directly referring to the protection of human rights.[1] These principles have been the foundation stone on which future progress in the field of human rights has proceeded since that date. In furtherance of these objectives, the United Nations has set up from

---

[1] The UN Charter includes these objectives: "To reaffirm faith in fundamental human rights, in the dignity and worth of the human person, in the equal rights of men and women and of nations large and small." (*Preamble*) "To achieve international cooperation in solving international problems of an economic, social, cultural, or humanitarian character, and in promoting and encouraging respect for human rights and for fundamental freedoms for all without distinction as to race, sex, language, or religion." (Chap. I., Art. I).

time to time special machinery to study and promote human rights on different levels.

The center of this action has been the Economic and Social Council (ECOSOC), one of the main organs of the UN and, especially, its Commission on Human Rights, which reports regularly to the Council and, through it, to the General Assembly, as the governing organ of the UN. Two other advisory bodies set up by ECOSOC to deal with human rights are a Sub-Commission on the Prevention of Discrimination and the Protecton of Minorities, and a Commission on the Status of Women. The work of these bodies will be referred to in later chapters. Through such organs as these the UN is able to fulfill its declared role as "a center for harmonizing the actions of nations" in the field of human rights.

THE DECLARATION IS BORN

There are various Specialized Agencies, which also report to ECOSOC. Among these latter are such Agencies as the ILO and UNESCO, which take a leading part in the furtherance of human rights, each within its own field of action. Reference will be made in later chapters to the part played by such specialized Agencies and other expert bodies in extending the scope and operation of human rights. It should be remembered that all these Commissions and other bodies report to ECOSOC and ultimately all these bodies report to the General Assembly which has the main overall responsibility. The Security Council has responsibility when violations of human rights threaten peace.

So much for the bare machinery. It was felt, however, that something spectacular should be done to concentrate world attention on what human rights really mean in the modern world and, by such a demonstration, to reveal how far short some national governments fell in upholding those rights. Hence, the Commission on Human Rights was charged with the difficult task of drawing up a comprehensive list of these rights, so that nobody could plead ignorance as to what they were.

This Commission, under the Chairmanship of the late Mrs. Eleanor Roosevelt, and composed of 18 members, came into existence in 1946 and held its first session in January 1947. Its duties were to submit proposals to ECOSOC regarding (a) an international bill of rights; (b) international declarations or conventions on civil libertes, the status of women, freedom of information, and similar matters; (c) the protection of minorities; (d) the prevention of discrimination on grounds of race, sex, language or religion, and (e) any other matters concerning human rights not covered by these items.

After many meetings and after receiving a mass of information and useful advice from all over the globe, a Universal Declaration of Human Rights was finally drafted by the Commission and presented to the UN General Assembly in 1948. On the 10th of December of that year, the General Assembly voted agreement with the principles set forth in the Declaration. 48 votes were in favor, *none* were against, and 8 nations abstained. Since that historic date, other nations have entered the UN; as they become members they automatically endorse the principles of the Declaration of Human Rights.

So, today, the Declaration may in truth be taken as the agreed policy of all the Member States since the agreed policy is in the UN Charter as ratified by all Member States. In the following chapters, we shall study the contents of this Declaration in four stages, but, at the same time, explain something of the other activities of the "UN Family" concerned with implementing the different items in the Declaration.

DISCUSSION SUGGESTIONS

1. Do you see any vital distinction between "declarations" made by one side in the course of a war—such as "The Four Freedoms" or "The Atlantic Charter"—and those which emerge from the agreement of many nations, not involved in military conflict with each other? What attitudes would you expect to find in the latter, which you would not find in the former case?

2. The Covenant of the League of Nations was an intrinsic part of the Treaty of Versailles, which concluded the First World War. Do you think it has been an advantage to have drafted the Charter of the UN as a distinct document, irrespective of any "peace" treaty terminating the Second World War? Has such a procedure aided the subsequent development of human rights principles embodied in the Charter?

CHAPTER III

The Universal Declaration of Human Rights

The Universal Declaration consists of 30 Articles. Although the language is simple—surprisingly simple for an official document, which needs to be expressed in precise language—every word has been the subject of many hours of thought and discussion by legal experts and national representatives, before being finally adopted by the UN Assembly. We could spend a good deal of time in studying each Article and trying to get behind the meanings of the words we find there. But, for the purpose of this booklet, all that can be done is to pick out the chief points and to comment on some of the leading ideas contained within these simple phrases. For—make no mistake about it—the Declaration is one of the most important documents of our time and embodies the hopes and aspirations of all human beings on this planet.

SURMOUNTING THE OBSTACLES

Actually, the Articles took over two years of hard work to put together on the part of the drafters, who tried to produce statements which could not be misunderstood, even when translated—as they have been—into many languages.

It has been said that "right", like "justice", is a word for which men have found it much easier to die than to define. One of the chief difficulties of the drafters was to find clear definitions which would fit every type of national culture. It is next to impossible to write laws which are the same in every country, where legal institutions and political traditions are different. It is even more difficult to get international action, which will apply equally to all countries. So it must first be understood that, in drawing up the Universal Declaration of

Human Rights, many obstacles had to be overcome so as to put into the same form of words definitions which would have the same meaning in the many cultures, religions, and political systems of the UN Member States.

Furthermore, some governments have taken the position that human rights can only be secured by passing new national laws and, therefore, it was futile to draw up an international declaration, which had no force of law at all in their own countries.

It was found necessary, to supplement the declaration by several conventions. The reason for drafting the conventions is that a declaration has no binding effect, whereas a convention establishes legal obligations upon those who ratify it. Then, again in countries which have a *federal* type of government—such as the United States or Australia—an additional problem arose because there are generally special procedures which regulate the signing of international treaties by a federal state. The United States, for example, which has frequently declared its adherence to the *principles* of human rights, has not ratified certain specific Conventions embodying those human rights in binding international agreements, such as the Genocide Convention. With all these obstacles to contend with, it is little short of a miracle that the Universal Declaration was drafted and accepted by so many countries in so short a time.

INDIVIDUAL COMES BEFORE THE STATE

The Declaration itself is introduced by a Preamble setting out in general terms (see Appendix I) the basic ideas which have been expanded later on in the main text. For instance, the Preamble says that "the inherent dignity" of each member of the human family is the starting point of the Declaration. So the *individual*, not the state or the nation or the government, is "the foundation of freedom, justice and peace in the world."

On the other hand, it goes on, "disregard and contempt for human rights have resulted in barbarous acts which have outraged the conscience of mankind". Because of this, it is essential "that human rights should be protected by the rule of law."

This assertion is plainly a direct challenge to all states—and they are many—which have not yet provided their peoples with this protection, either by introducing the necessary laws or establishing that machinery of justice that will enforce these

14

laws equally among all their inhabitants. For the "rule of law" means that everybody counts for one.

The Preamble goes on to state that the Declaration is based on the Charter of the United Nations, in which the Member States "have pledged themselves to achieve, in co-operation with the UN, the promotion of universal respect for and observance of human rights and fundamental freedoms." Yet it is recognized tht it is not sufficient for the General Assembly of the UN merely to have proclaimed the Declaration as "a common standard of achievement for all peoples and all nations." Every individual in the world, and all governments and groups, are urged to strive, "by teaching and education," to promote these rights in every way that is open to them among the peoples of the Member States and all other peoples within their influence.

This is a most sweeping appeal. It leaves no one any excuse to think that the responsibility for observing the terms of the Declaration is a job to be left to somebody else. That is what is meant by "universal."

NEED FOR A COVENANT

But one important question of drafting remains. Is a proclamation of this kind—however widely accepted by "We, the Peoples"—enough to ensure that its principles will be embodied in the national laws? The answer is: No. General declarations, however emphatic they may be, do not legally commit governments until accepted by them in the form of an international treaty. Treaties may be broken, of course—and often are—but they do represent, up to this point of time, the strongest form of binding obligation on nations and on their governments. So it was agreed, even while the Declaration was being drafted (so as not to delay its completion) that a treaty to protect human rights should also be drafted and put before the world's governments for signature and ratification, embodying and amplifying the ideas of the Declaration. Thus, the full force of international law would be put behind them.

The name frequently given to this kind of treaty between sovereign states is "covenant." So an International Covenant on Human Rights was decided upon. Discussions in the General Assembly showed, however, that it would be preferable to prepare two separate covenants: one on civil and political rights, and the other on economic, social and cultural rights. Preliminary drafts were completed in 1954 and the Economic and Social Council passed them on to the General Assembly for final drafting and adoption.

Space need not be devoted here to following their progress, but the Third Committee of the General Assembly (which deals with social questions) has recently completed practically all the substantive Articles of both Covenants. Where necessary, comments will be made on the Articles so adopted later in this pamphlet. When ratified by the required number of States, these Convenants or treaties will be legally binding on States which are parties to them. Meantime, an examination of some of the chief articles of the Declaration will take us into the subject matter of these Covenants.

HUMAN BROTHERHOOD

Article 1 states quite simply that "all human beings are born free and equal in dignity and rights." Because of this fact, they "should act towards one another in a spirit of brotherhood." Thus, for the first time, an international instrument, universally accepted, proclaims the principle of human brotherhood, which has been enshrined for hundreds of years in the great religions of the world and in the books of the philosophers.

It will be recalled that terms similar to those in Article 1 have been included in some of the great national documents of the modern world. The American Declaration of Independence, of 1776, begins: "We hold these truths to be self evident, that all men are created equal; that they are endowed by their Creator with certain inalienable rights; that among these are life, liberty, and the pursuit of happiness." In the French Declaration of the Rights of Man in 1789 (incorporated in 1791 in the French Constitution) we read: "Men are born free and remain free and with equal rights". But such assertions as these are national in their origin and scope. The national unit alone can no longer guarantee the fullest measure of human freedom.

The two sentences of this article hang together. To simplify their meaning further, they can be reversed as follows: "*Because* all people on earth are brothers and sisters and form one human family, they must respect and help one another in every

16

way they can." Could anything be clearer—as a way of life for *all* mankind?

OVERCOMING PREJUDICE

The second Article carries the premise further. It is quite general and states, in part, that "everyone is entitled to all the rights and freedoms set forth in this Declaration, without distinction of any kind . . . "Then it lists a number of categories in which men are frequently divided and insists that, because of the principle laid down in Article 1, these categories—race, color, sex, language, religion and so on—must no longer affect any individual's rights.

This is another way of saying that discrimination on the ground of any of these physical or social differences is prohibited. No human being is to be treated differently because he differs from his fellows in these aspects of his life, because of his appearance, or because of his views. In other words, a man's personal *rights* on this planet have nothing to do with his family or his ancestors, the color of his skin, the language he speaks, his wealth or possessions, or his poverty in worldly goods.

It is obvious that some governments do not always live up to these standards! But this principle of non-discrimination is beginning to be recognized. When the yardstick of this Article is set against their recent conduct, many nations, with vastly differing political structures, are brought before the bar of public opinion at the United Nations and openly criticised and condemned for practicing or condoning discrimination.

DISCUSSION SUGGESTIONS

1. Is it a fact that men are "born free"? Why do you think the drafters of Article 1 employ the verb "are born equal," instead of "should be" equal? Notice how the words "should act" come into the second sentence. Why was the article worded in this way?

2. Outlined the facts of a situation known to you, in your neighborhood or organization, where distinctions are being made between people on any of the grounds specified in Article 2. What is being done to rectify the situation?

CHAPTER IV

Freedom Of The Individual

Articles 3 to 11 center upon the freedom of the individual, and they form the main subject of this chapter.

Article 3 begins: "Everyone has the right to life." This may look like a simple phrase, but it will become clearer during the course of the following pages that the life of the individual requires quite an elaborate piece of social machinery to look after it. It has, in fact, taken many centuries to establish the right to life. That is why so much time has been given at United Nations meetings to describe or define the various methods which different nations have adopted to ensure this basic human right, or —which is more often the case—to deny it.

Article 3 reads in its entirety: "Everyone has the right to life, liberty and security of person." But, when the Social Committee of the General Assembly came to discuss this Article, after it had been embodied some years later in the draft Covenant of Human Rights, the Committee spent over a dozen meetings analysing what the "right to life" *really means.* As a result, proposals were made to the UN Assembly, and afterwards adopted by it, which expanded the above simple sentence to a considerable degree. If we look, therefore, at what that UN Committee discussed, we shall realise that defending the "right to life" is by no means such an easy question as it seems to be at first sight.

OUR RIGHT TO STAY ALIVE

How can a man's natural desire to stay alive be protected by his nation's law? That was the issue which caused so many weeks of discussion in the autumn of 1957, and again in 1959, when the Third Committee attempted to find a form of words to implement the Article legally. We shall take this special example a little further in this chapter, though it should be borne in mind that, if space permitted, many of the Declaration's other articles would tell a similar story.

The extraordinary thing about the 1957 and 1959 debates is that *all* the national delegations agreed that the "right to life" existed. What they differed about was: under what conditions could that "right" *be taken away* by the state? In other words, on what grounds could the state legitimately deprive a person of his life—and yet observe the terms of the Declaration? Here was a conundrum. For it is well known that the death penalty has been part of national laws from time immemorial.

In the course of the debate, it was revealed that over twenty states had already *abolished* capital punishment by law, while another twenty or so never or rarely practiced it. So these states had little difficulty with being categorical about the right to life. Moreover, some of them—Uruguay and Colombia, for instance—tried very hard to convince the other delegations that their way was the *only* way consistent with the Declaration. Yet they were defeated when it came to vote.

The other states argued that it was impossible to postulate that basic right so boldly. It had to be hedged around with exceptions, because mankind was not yet perfect, and bad people—murderers in particular—had to be deterred by the threat of death.

Those debates make very interesting reading for the serious student of social institutions; but they covered too many questions of philosophy, law, and penal reform to be included here. But, at the end of it all, the Committee agreed on a form of words, the gist of which is as follows:

> Every human being has the inherent right to life. This right shall be protected by law. No one shall be arbitrarily deprived of his life.
>
> In countries which have not abolished the death penalty, sentence of death may be imposed only for the most serious crimes in accordance with law in force at the time of the commission of the crime. . . .
>
> Anyone sentenced to death shall have the right to seek pardon or commutation of the sentence. Amnesty, pardon or commutation of the sentence of death may be granted in all cases.

Sentence of death shall not be imposed for crimes committed by persons below eighteen years of age and shall not be carried out on pregnant women.

Nothing in this article shall be invoked to delay or to prevent the abolition of capital punishment by any State Party to the Covenant.

It will be noted that, by the last sentence, the Committee left the door open in a very diplomatic fashion for any state, which at present practices capital punishment, to change its laws and abolish the penalty, and so get rid of all the exceptions which form the bulk of the text finally agreed upon. Thus, a form of words was found—and later accepted by a large majority of the UN Assembly—which put Article 3 into due legal form.

WHAT IS GENOCIDE?

Yet two important matters still remained. The first was the need felt by many states to bring a reference to "genocide" into the text and outline procedures of punishment. Genocide means "race-killing"—that is, the intentional destruction of human *groups*. Genocide was declared to be a crime under international law by the resolution of the General Assembly in 1946, and a Convention was unanimously adopted by the Assembly two years later.

This Convention defines "genocide" as the commitment of acts with the object of destroying, in whole or in part, a national, ethnic, racial or religious group—that is to say, by aiming at the group as such, not at individuals as individuals. Acts constituting genocide are killing, causing serious bodily or mental harm, deliberately inflicting conditions of life calculated to bring about physical destruction of a group, imposing measures intended to prevent birth, and the forceable transfer of children. Not only genocide itself is declared an international crime, but also conspiracy or incitement to commit it, are punishable under the Convention.

Then the Genocide Convention goes on to insist that *all* who are guilty of genocide must be punished "whether they are constitutionally responsible rulers, public officers or private individuals." In other words, no one can hide behind his own government after this, or use the excuse that he acted on "superior orders," if his acts constitute the international crime of genocide. It yet remains to be seen how this important new world law will work out in practice.

The purpose of the Convention is to prevent, or to deter from ever recurring, the atrocious acts of extermination of whole peoples, which were witnessed especially during the Second World War, and which played a prominent part in the Nuremburg war-crime trials. The text of the draft Convention on Human Rights included, therefore, a direct reference to the earlier Genocide Convention, to the effect that "when deprivation of life constitutes the crime of genocide, it is understood that nothing in this Article shall authorize any State Party to derogate in any way from any obligation assumed under the provisions of the Convention on the Prevention and Punishment of the Crime of Genocide."

DEATH PENALTY COMES UNDER FIRE

The other matter which came out of this elaborate examination of the meaning of Article 3, rang a more positive note. On the advice of the Committee, the UN Assembly proposed in 1959 that a thorough study should be made of that big exception to the right to life—the death penalty. The UN Secretariat was charged with the task of preparing a detailed report on the *pros* and *cons* of this form of ultimate punishment. A set of questions was sent to all governments, and, on the basis of the replies from over 60 of them and from non-governmental organizations interested in criminal reform and expert lawyers and crimnologists, a report was drawn up and issued in the spring of 1963, which, for the first time, brings together a worldwide survey of this important branch of criminal law.

What will emerge, when this momentous report is put before the UN Assembly, after being examined by ECOSOC, nobody knows. But the arduous researches and discussions carried out by the UN, in order to make clear to everybody what the first five words of Article 3 really *mean*, has been presented here as a concrete example of how seriously many people are beginning to regard the obligations imposed on them and on their governments by the Universal Declaration of Human Rights.

ALL FORMS OF SLAVERY PROHIBITED

Arising from man's primary right to keep his own life secure,

21

a large number of other rights follow. These are set out in the Articles 4 to 11. Only brief comments can be made on the chief of them in the remainder of this chapter. If we turn to the text in Appendix 1, we note how these articles all relate closely together.

Naturally, slavery "in all its forms" (Article 4) can have no part in civilized society. Some people of the Western world are surprised to learn that slavery still exists in some Middle East territories, and in some spots of Asia and Africa. But the UN Assembly—that open forum of world opinion—has again and again had its attention drawn to the actual details of this hideous institution existing in dark places of the earth.

The history of the international fight against slavery is a continuous one and several anti-slavery conventions—going back to the original League of Nations Slavery Convention of 1926—have been adopted. These conventions, prohibit slavery in all of its forms, and also outlaw institutions and practices similar to slavery, such as debt bondage, serfdom, bride-price and the exploitation of child labor.

But the whole "UN Family" is engaged in the world struggle over Human Rights. This is shown by the powerful attack which is being made on what is called "forced labor," a form of servitude imposed upon individuals by governments rather than by individuals. Here, the International Labor Office (ILO) has had a direct part in investigating working conditions in various countries, leading up to the adoption, in June 1957, of its Convention on the Abolition of Forced Labor. Under this Convention, States Parties undertake to supress any form of forced or compulsory labor whether it is used (a) as a means of political coercion or education, or as punishment for holding or expressing political views; (b) as a method of mobilizing labor for purposes of economic developments; (c) as a method of labor discipline; (d) as a punishment for having participated in strikes; or (e) as a means of racial, social, national or religious discrimination. This is a very sweeping Convention—and yet one more attempt to underpin the Universal Decalartion by international law.[1]

---

[1] For further details of the foregoing aspects of the UN's campaign for Human Rights, see the UN pamphlet: "UN Work for Human Rights" (pp. 15-19) and the pamphlet in this Study Guide Series: "The Human Needs of Labor."

PUNISHMENT MUST FIT THE CRIME

Articles 5 and 11 bear mainly on the subject of punishment for crime.

"No one shall be subjected to torture" (Article 5), goes almost without saying in the 20th century. But is it not important to state it afresh? "Cruel, inhuman or degrading treatment or punishment" cannot be outlawed too quickly, even in so-called "civilized" countries. Hence, Article 11 lays down that punishment can only be meted out *after* a public trial and *after* the accused has been proved guilty "according to law"; and, even then, the punishment must fit the crime. In other words of the later Article: "nor shall a heavier penalty be imposed than the one that was applicable at the time the penal offence was committed." This is a warning against *ex post facto law*—law that has been enacted after the offence has been committed.

The other Articles surveyed here, from 6 to 10, all enforce the "Rule of Law," explained in Chapter III—everybody counts for one. This principle is clearly stated, for instance, in Article 6: "Everyone has the right to recognition everywhere as a person before the law." The other articles mentioned will bear careful study, as they contain within them many of the historical landmarks of human freedom.

A DAY IN COURT

In fact, these articles are so important, that the effectiveness of the whole Declaration rests upon them. As lawyers sometimes express it: "The remedy precedes the right." This means that, *unless* a man has an independent and impartial authority to protect his rights and redress his wrongs, in the last resort, he is lost. This idea is more popularly put: "Everyone is entitled to his day in Court."

Hence, the court or tribunal must be *just*, and it must be efficient. The accused person must not be arrested "arbitrarily" (Article 9)—that is, without a reason that can stand up in a court of law. And, when he is brought before the court, he must have all the facilities and professional help he needs for his defense. He is entitled to an "independent and impartial" tribunal (Article 10), i.e. a tribunal which has no interest in the outcome of the case, except to see that justice is done according to the law

23

in force at the time of the alleged offense.

Why all these safeguards? Why all this care—even to protect a man who may turn out to be a convicted criminal? The answer is contained in Article 11. Every individual "has the right to be presumed innocent *until proven guilty*." This principle is the basis of freedom before the law. It is a criterion of a nation's degree of civilization. Without it, there can be no justice between man and man, and consequently, no stability for society. In this principle, upheld before the eyes of the whole world by the Universal Declaration, is the essence of the dignity of man.

DISCUSSION SUGGESTIONS

1. When Rosseau began his book on *The Social Contract* with the words: "Man is born free, but everywhere he is in chains," what do you think he meant to convey? Give examples of different forms of slavery of past times. Do you know of any cases of such slavery existing today?

2. Is conscription of citizens for war a form of slavery or forced labor? How would you define it under the terms of the Declaration?

3. Has the state a "right" to take human life? If so, in what circumstances? Does the Declaration restrict the imposition of the death penalty? Why have some states abolished capital punishment? Give examples.

4. Outline the safeguards which you think a person accused of a crime should have in a court of law, under the terms of the Declaration. What do people mean by "trial by newspaper?" Is is true that "only the rich get away with murder"?

CHAPTER V

Civil And Political Rights

From the individual, we now turn to the home. Article 12 begins a new series of rights spreading ever wider from the family unit to the political unit—the state—where, as Article 21 puts it: "Everyone has the right of equal access to public service in his country." Between Articles 12 and 21 (to which this chapter will be devoted), the rights of the individual can be seen expanding, as it were, into a series of concentric circles, each gaining much from the other.

For example, the point of Article 12, which lays down the rule that every man's home shall be "his castle"—i.e. no outsider shall be allowed to interfere with it—is strengthened by Article 16, asserting his "right to marry and to found a family." These two articles, therefore, will be considered together.

THE 4 A.M. KNOCK

How often has it happened in the all-too-recent past, that the "4 a.m. knock" on the door has meant arbitrary arrest and imprisonment—the destruction at one blow of all human rights—by a dictatorship? Could any right, involving, as Article 12 says, "protection of the law against such interference and attacks," be more essential to man's very existence in society?

Yet, this Article goes further and insists that his "privacy" and his "correspondence"—and that includes his telephone!—and even his "honour and reputation" are to be protected from any intruder or outsider, whether government or private person.

Article 16 adds a very good reason for this element of "sacredness." It states that "the family is the natural and fundamental group unit of society"—a fact that is too ofen overlooked by political philosophers. Hence, a man's family "is entitled to protection by society and the State." In conformity with this principle of co-operation between the sexes, the point of the very first Article of the Declaration is taken up once again and emphasized in the phrase: "Men and women . . . are entitled to equal rights as to marriage." A person's sex is never to be the test to a person's civic rights.

Need it be stressed that the United Nations has devoted a great deal of energy to vindicating this modern concept of marriage? In many parts of the world, long-ingrained national customs and legal institutions have never recognized such equality in the partnership of marriage. The infliction on women of legal and social inferiority has been a constant source of struggle and conflict, not merely in terms of the marriage contract, but—as later articles testify—in relation to education, property rights, political status, and much else.

CHAMPION OF WOMEN'S RIGHTS

The UN General Assembly has already—thanks often to the initiative of the women members of its Social Committee and other advisory bodies, such as the Human Rights Commission and the Commission on the Status of Women—tackled the problems of the legal equality of the sexes. In 1957, the Convention on the Nationality of Married Women was adopted. This Convention protects women from the automatic loss of acquisition of nationality because of marriage to a man of a different nationality. Later a Convention on Consent to Marriage, Minimum Age of Marriage, and Registration of Marriage was adopted in 1962 to eliminate such practices as child marriage, bride-price and the inheritance of widows, which are still prevalent in some parts of the world, as mentioned in Chapter IV. This Convention also provides that no marriage shall be legally entered into without the full and free consent of both spouses, that both parties shall have reached the minimum age specified by law, and that all marriages shall be officially registered.

Similarly, a Convention on the Political Rights of Women, to ensure that women obtain political oportunities and status equal to those enjoyed by men, was adopted by the General Assembly in 1952. This Convention requires states which have ratified it to grant women the right to vote, to be elected to and to hold public office, and to carry out public functions on equal terms with

26

men. It will thus be seen that Article 16 is—and will obviously remain—a live issue for a long time to come.

These are concrete examples of how, with the principles of the Declaration as a guide post, more and more agreements are being arrived at between nations of widely differing cultures and institutions. Gradually, national deficiencies are being brought up to the international standard. Women are themselves, of course, among the world leaders in the vindication of their rights.

PASSPORTS AND FUGITIVES

Residence comes up again in Article 13. But this time we are looking outward rather than inward. Outside "his castle," the modern citizen "has the right to freedom of movement," not merely within his own state, but also "to leave any country" and to return to it if it is his own country. This is a bold affirmation, in view of the rivalries, suspicions and hostile attitudes which often exist between nations today. How far from the ideal—for it certainly is that—laid dawn in Article 13 is the practice, if not the national laws, of many states! It is not possible here to embark on a detailed discussion of passports, visas, and other travel "authorizations." These cumbersome documents have tended to become, in effect, restrictions on, rather than aids to travel and free movement. Yet, in the absence of such, millions of less fortunate individuals have no escape from their predicament. The point of Article 13 is that freedom of movement has at least been *proclaimed* as a universal right.

Coming close on the heels of this magnificent vision of free movement across our common globe, we pass into the tragic area of the "lost people"—people "without a country" to belong to. These sad outcasts are the refugees and the stateless. Article 14 deals with the "right of asylum": in other words, the right of every individual (except those accused of political crimes) who has fled from his own country because, for example, his political opinions have put his life in danger, to be harboured and protected by the land to which he has fled. Behind this Article lies, of course, one of the oldest histories of "man's inhumanity to man." Only a short summary of the UN's continuous effort on behalf of this vast kingdom of the lost—reckoned as at least 40 million people, following the Second World War—can be attempted here.

The United Nations has been studying statelessness and related questions since 1947. Under its auspices, several Conventions protecting the rights of refugees and stateless persons, have already been adopted, and a High Commissioner for Refugees was appointed to assist refugees with their problems.

In July 1951, for example, a Convention on the Status of Refugees was adopted by the General Assembly. It entered into force in April 1954. Some 27 states have ratified or acceded to this Convention. The parties to the Convention undertake to give to refugees the same treatment as nationals with regard to religion, access to courts, elementary education, social security, and so on. Provision is also made for issuing travel documents to refugees and protecting them from expulsion from the country of refuge. In 1960 during the World Refugee Year campaign, an attempt was made to liquidate the refugee camps in Europe and elsewhere, but many tens of thousands still remain in those camps.

A Convention relating to the Status of Stateless Persons was adopted in 1954 and came into force on June 6, 1960, after eight governments had ratified it or acceded to it. This Convention is based on the Refugees Convention, and States party to it undertake to grant to stateless persons almost the same standards of treatment as to refugees. A stateless person is defined as "a person who is not considered as a national by any state under the operation of its law."

Then, more recently, on the agenda of the General Assembly has come a draft declaration on the right of asylum, prepared by the Commission on Human Rights in 1960. The draft declaration is an atempt to set forth general principles by which states and the international community should be guided in granting asylum. It says that asylum granted by a state shall be respected by all other states. Persons forced to leave a country "because of persecution or well-founded fear of persecution" are a matter of concern to the international community. No one seeking asylum should (except for such reasons as national security) be subjected to measures such as rejection at the frontier, return and expulsion, which would result in compelling him to return or to remain in a country where his life might be threatened. That is where we must leave the steady progress of Article 14 at this moment of time; but the fact that the lonely fugitive has become "of concern to the international community" is a milestone to progress.

In spite of this different problem of securing recognition of the rights of a man seeking political asylum the next article, Article 15, insists that "everyone has the right to a nationality." The language is explicit. And, as a corollary, the second part of the Article states that no one shall be "deprived of his nationality." Nevertheless, he may change it, if he desires.

This again—bearing in mind the known practices of some states --may look like a vague and distant ideal. Yet Article 15 has already been cited in court actions—in Italy in 1954 for example —as a persuasive *principle* of "the highest moral value." Such a standard of natural justice can be ignored only to the loss of the state which rejects it.

We have referred to Article 16 earlier in the chapter.

PRIVATE—KEEP OFF!

Little need be said about Article 17, which states that "everyone has the right to own property." This seems a fairly obvious proposition to most people, yet the right to own property has been a disputed principle over the centuries. The gist of the right is really to be found in the second sentence, which lays down that no one shall be *arbitrarily* deprived of his property. The point of this qualification is that, where private property is taken over compulsorily by the civil authorities—as it often is in the course of the economic or social planning of the community— compensation must be paid for it, which a court of law would consider to be reasonable in all the circumstances.

Articles 18 and 19 both take us back to that important objective mentioned in the Preamble of the UN Charter itself: "to practice tolerance." But notice how both these articles have two sides to them. "Freedom of thought, conscience, and religion" (Article 18)and "freedom of opinion" (Article 19)—yes, true; but that sort of freedom exists inside of us. Who can tell what goes on in a man's mind—in his "heart," as we say?

So it would not mean much if the articles stopped there. It is the second part of both articles which breaks new ground and —as they are doing—challenges the habits of many governments.

For a personal belief or opinion to be truly "free," it must be expressible publicly. Hence the emphasis in Article 18 is on "manifest"—"manifest his religion or belief in teaching, practice, worship, and observance"—all public actions. And the point is taken further in Article 19, because everyone may enjoy "without interference," the freedom "to seek, receive and impart information and ideas through any media and regardless of frontiers."

COMPLEX PROBLEMS

Merely to cite the words of these two important articles is to show into what complicated areas the clear-cut principles of the Declaration have moved. Freedom of the press, of radio, of political opposition, of minority groups—how many countries can one list within recent memory which seem to care nothing for this kind of freedom? The United Nations has devoted many meetings recently to the methods and techniques involved in promoting freedom of information within and between countries. It is sadly the case that not only the authoritarian states have put difficulties in the way of improving such facilities.[1]

Who makes up the mind, the ideology, of a nation or people? Article 19 opens up the whole complex field of political organization. It asks, in effect: "Who is the State?" Is it "We the People" —where everyone has, and exercises without interference, the right to free opinion? Or does the State consist of a group or even an individual who says, with Louis XIV, *"L'état c'est moi"*—I am the State?

It will thus be seen that the simple, direct phrases of the Declaration go far beyond a prescription for personal freedom. They lay down the essential conditions of how a state should be organized so that all its citizens may "count for one," whatever their benefits or opinions may be.

FREEDOM FOR JOINERS

The next two articles, which conclude the present chapter, follow on naturally from this concept. The first of them, Article 20, says that anyone has a right to *join* any association or organ-

---

[1] This important topic is too complicated to be outlined above; but a summary of the activities of the UN bodies in this field can be found in the UN pamphlet "UN Work for Human Rights" (pp. 19-21).

ization, but no one can *make him* join it if he doesn't want to. There is one qualification, however, for "joiners." Their meetings must have peaceful objectives. That seems only reasonable.

This article enshrines, among other things, the basic principle of our trade unions. The Economic and Social Council has worked in close co-operation with the ILO for the promotion of trade union rights since 1947, and, as a result of this co-operation, the International Labor Conference adopted in 1948 the Freedom of Association and Protection of the Right to Organize Convention, and, in 1949, the Right to Organize and Collective Bargaining Convention. The ILO has also established machinery for the examination of attacks on trade union rights. Such allegations are forwarded to the Governing Body of that organization, and often are debated in the plenary session of the ILO Conference.

Many other Conventions of the ILO—going back to 1919, when the ILO was founded—further ensure this freedom. In fact, a vast range of national and international legislation, called the World Labor Code, has been the outcome of this principle. Millions of workers in all countries owe to these Conventions better standards of health, pay, working conditions, social security benefits, and trade union progress. "Freedom of association" has become the badge of the modern worker, whatever his job or nationality.

THE WILL OF THE PEOPLE

Article 21 reads something like an essay in political democracy. The will of the people, says the article, is "the basis of the authority of government." Every people has the right to choose its own government. There should be free, secret and periodic elections on the basis of "universal and equal suffrage." Everyone has "the right to take part in the government of his country" and "the right of equal access to public service in his country."

Could anything bring government and governed more closely together? Could our short study of civil and political rights of the Declaration end on a more positive note than this—that government shall rest on "the will of the people"?

DISCUSSION SUGGESTIONS

1. Should a foreigner be as free to move about in a country as

a citizen? Should passports be abolished? If so, what would be some of the consequences? Should right of asylum be freely granted to *anyone* who applies for it?

2. At what point does property become "public"? Should schools, town-halls, bridges, railways, ships, radio-systems, be owned by private persons? Do you think that Article 17 (1) adequately expresses the right to own property as exercised in your own country?

3. What do we mean by "freedom of the press"? Who controls the press in your country? How could mass media be democratically organized?

CHAPTER VI

Economic, Social, and Cultural Rights

The word "ideal" has already come into these chapters several times. The rights thus far described are standards, challenges, ideals—let all this be admitted. But, even so, the evidence grows daily that, without the, life on this planet would indeed be, in the words of the political philosopher, Thomas Hobbes, "dark, brutish and short." A similar point has been made by an older and perhaps wiser sage:

"Where there is no vision, the people perish."

It is necessary to begin this chapter—which surveys Articles 22 to 27—in this manner, because these half-dozen articles, taken together, read like a panorama of a very distant landscape. Turning to these six articles (and they take barely that number of minutes to read thoughtfully and deliberately), we are presented with a contrast to our present world which—even as far as some "advanced" countries are concerned—make it very hard for us to feel encouraged. Against the human misery and hunger and deprivation which exists at this moment across, possibly, two-thirds of the earth's surface, the shining ideals contained in these paragraphs look so other-worldly, as to be outside the bounds of reality.

BRIDGING THE CHASM

And yet, as we look closer, we notice that many rights included in this list of economic, social and cultural rights are already shared by millions of citizens in some of the "advanced" countries. Take Article 22, for instance, which speaks of "the right to social security." It then goes on to assert that "the organization and resources of each State" should back up this right. In some countries there is a close approximation to this ideal. But, once again, it is the chasm which exists today between the "have" and "have-not" nations, which lies between two quite different practices of human rights. That is one reason why the article links together "national effort and international co-operation."[1]

Social security depends on two factors, above all others: national economic prosperity and adequate machinery to administer it. Economic standards of life are reflected in prevailing social standards; but, even so, there can be vast disparities between rich people and poor people within a relatively flourishing state. So, here, one of the basic principles of the whole Declaration—EQUALITY—comes in once again. Economic prosperity must be shared by all the citizens. For *everyone*, not just a lucky few, is entitled to enjoy the economic, social and cultural rights "indispensable for his dignity and the free development of his personality."

IDEALS INTO REALITY

The important social rights described in Articles 23 and 24 have already been dealt with in some detail in another pamphlet in this series,[1] so a broad summary must suffice here. They cover different aspects of employment, each of which has been set out in considerable detail in many ILO Conventions.

We saw, at the beginning of this pamphlet, that, whereas the Declaration lays down principles, the *application* of these principles, amidst all the complexity of national and international affairs, has usually to be ensured by state laws and international agreements in the form of Conventions. This is particularly true of labor legislation, since the working conditions which prevail in one country—seeing that they are directly related to the economic prosperity of that country—affect the working conditions in neighboring areas. This happens either through the operation of trade competition or through the co-operation of trade unions, which nowadays have powerful international organizations to safeguard their rights. The last sentence of Article 23 reads: "Everyone has the right to form and to join trade unions for the protection of his interests."

Basically, "the right to work," with which Article 23 begins,

---

[1] See the Study Guide in this series, "The Human Needs of Labor," for specific facts on the way the ILO has been implementing this Article and the next following ones.

34

carries with it all the other rights specified: "free choice of employment" and "protection against unemployment," "equal pay for equal work," "remuneration ensuring . . . an existence worthy of human dignity," and, even (Article 24) "holidays with pay." Yet these were once—not so long ago—explosive phrases in the advancing industrial countries! Now, they have become normal world-accepted standards. So need we despair of the remoteness of such "ideals" from present reality?

FROM BIRTH TO OLD AGE

Again we are back with the family unit. Article 25 takes up from where Article 16 left off, for in the latter article our concern was with the legal and civic rights of the family. The first part of the present article lists a large number of essential requirements to which the modern family is entitled: "food, clothing, housing, and medical care and necessary social services." Such elements of normal life are included to encourage governments to discharge all their moral obligations with regard to the principles of the Declaration. Sickness and disability benefits—mentioned here—are too often left to chance, or to the meagre resources of the sufferer, by even some modern democratic administrations. The right to security in widowhood and old age, specified in the Article, is still a long way from being implemented by these same administrations.

"Motherhood and childhood are entitled to special care and assistance," reads the second part of Article 25. Here it can be recalled that, in 1959, the UN General Assembly unanimously adopted a Declaration on the Rights of the Child. The Declaration states that the child, by reason of his physical and mental immaturity is entitled to special safeguards and care, before as well as after birth. It affirms that mankind owes to the child the best it has to give. Parents, individuals, voluntary organizations, local authorities and governments are all called upon to recognize the rights and freedoms of children and to strive for their observance in their own countries. But, in addition to the right of all children to enjoy special protection and to be given opportunities and facilities to enable them to develop in a healthy manner and in conditions of freedom and dignity, to have a name and a nationality from birth and to enjoy the benefits of adequate nutrition, housing, recreation and medical services, the Declara-

35

tion also emphasizes that the child shall be brought up "in a spirit of understanding, tolerance, friendship among peoples, peace and universal brotherhood and in full consciousness that his energy and talents should be devoted to the service of his fellow men."

FREEDOM AND COMPULSION

It will be noticed how many of the other aspects of the work of the UN's Economic and Social Council (ECOSOC) come into this chapter. The ILO, as one of the Specialized Agencies, has already been seen in operation as the international "umbrella" organization, protecting the human rights of labor in many fields. Similarly, the United Nations Educational, Scientific and Cultural Organization (UNESCO) becomes the background working organizations behind Articles 26 and 27, with which this Chapter closes. Another pamphlet in this series provides an outline guide to UNESCO's widely-flung activities on behalf of human rights in education, so, these final paragraphs will be confined to one or two essential comments by way of emphasis.[2]

Two phrases in Article 26 look a little startling at first: "Education shall be free, at least in the elementary and fundamental stages," and "Elementary education shall be compulsory." Yet, how can everyone have "the right to education," unless it is *provided* by the state or community, irrespective of the individual's, or his family's income? And how can *everybody* be assured of an education, unless his right is enforced even on himself?

TRUE END OF EDUCATION

These stipulations are doubtless controversial and have, in some countries at earlier stages of social development, led to bitter disputes. Yet the fact is that all the principles stated in Article 26 have been achieved in many Education Departments in the world and are the objectives of all. The basic problem in the developing countries is not how to evade any of them, but how to raise the necessary finance and carry out the *planning* of education, so that each one of these "ideals" becomes reality in the shortest possible time.

---

[2] See the Study Guide in this series: *Building Peace in the Minds of Men*, particularly Chapter VI on "Mutual Comprehension and Human Rights."

Educational planning is nowadays proceeding under the motto: "Every child in the world must have a school to go to by 1970." Yet planned education is not incompatible with the freedoms presented in this article. On the contrary, without these freedoms as an incentive and an objective, it is doubtful whether the national planning of education would carry along with it the enthusiasm and support of the many governments of Asia, Africa, and Latin America which, under the initiative of UNESCO, have committed themselves to its realization.

In another area, the UN Commission on the Status of Women, for instance, has been much concerned with the question of the access of women to education, especially in those countries where the status of women leaves much to be desired. In co-operation with UNESCO and the ILO, studies have been made on the access of girls and women to education at all levels and to the teaching profession and other professional training. Many programs of UNESCO are of special importance to women, such as projects aimed at increasing the participation of girls and women in education in the developing countries. In line with this policy, UNESCO recently adopted a comprehensive Convention providing for action to be taken against discrimination in education.[3]

Finally, the main point of Article 27, that "everyone has the right freely to participate in the cultural life of the community," is surely a corollary of the standard just laid down in the previous article that all "education should be directed to the full development of the human personality." In a cogent summing-up of all that has gone before in this chapter, Article 26 proclaims that the objective of such education is that it "shall promote understanding, tolerance, and friendship among all nations, racial, or religious groups, and shall further the activities of the United Nations for the maintenance of peace."

DISCUSSION SUGGESTIONS

1. Why has "social security" such a bad name in certain quarters? What items of daily living should be assured by state or municipal social security benefits? Do some forms of social se-

---

[3] See complete text of this Convention in the aforementioned pamphlet.

curity add to or detract from a recipient's "dignity and the free development of his personality"?

2. Why does the Declaration place such emphasis on the family unit? What are the benefits of the Universal Declaration with regard to the Rights of the Child? Are there dangers in national governments paying too much attention to the upbringing and instruction of children?

3. Why does the Declaration make primary education compulsory? Is this compatible with the other freedoms in the Declaration? Write down, in five or six sentences, what to you appear to be the marks of an educated person.

CHAPTER VII

The Supremacy of The Individual

In this brief chapter, which covers the last three articles of the Declaration, no new rights are introduced. But some important viewpoints are stressed which are tersely summed up in Article 29 by the phrase: "general welfare in a democratic society." Perhaps the word "welfare" has recently suffered an eclipse in certain quarters by being associated with a namby-pamby paternalism—i.e. the State will do *everything* for us! But this is not the scheme of things outlined in these last three articles.

MEANS WHAT IT SAYS

Article 30 may be disposed of straight away. It consists of a general safeguard frequently inserted at the tail-end of constitutional or formal documents, intended to deter any unfriendly "state, group, or person," from employing the *words* of the Declaration to defeat its obvious objectives. Admitting that the interpretation of legal terms is often difficult, the Declaration is worded to safeguard against any attempt toward nullifying the Declaration either by groups or by any person using his freedom to endanger the freedom of others.

But, to compensate for this apparent vagueness, our eye should travel higher to the last sentence in the previous article, Article 29. Here is given the best yardstick by which any distortion of the Declaration can always be checked: "These rights and freedoms may in no case be exercised contrary to the purposes and principles of the United Nations."

CHANGE MUST COME

The other two articles, however, bring us to some deeper

thoughts. Article 28 links the "social" to the "international" order. Legal and political organizations are important, and the bulk of the foregoing pages has borne out that opinion in some detail. But no society can remain static, and survive. Change is a law of life—collective as well as individual life. It cannot be denied that both the social order and the international order, still prevailing in many parts of the earth, make the rights surveyed in these pages impossible of achievement.

Hence, reads the article: "Everyone is entitled to a social and international order in which the rights and freedoms set forth in this Declaration can be fully realized." And, if this implies that man must change existing society—nationally or internationally—then change it he must!

SELF-DETERMINATION BECOMES A RIGHT

One vital topic can be referred to here, though there is hardly a word about it in the Declaration. When (see page 16) the two Covenants on Civil and Political Rights, on the one hand, and Economic Social and Cultural Rights, on the other hand, came before the General Assembly and its Social Committee, an entirely new section was grafted, as it were, on the original Human Rights stem in order to relate to the right of "self determination" set forth in the United Nations Charter. That addition—which has since had wide reverberations throughout the United Nations—can best be expressed in the term: "The right of peoples and nations to self-determination."

This principle in the approach to human rights, as evidenced in the present pamphlet, takes us into the controversial but vastly important field of the liquidation of "colonialism" in all its forms —political, economic, military. Many long and often acrimonious debates in the Assembly and other UN bodies testify as to the strength of conflicting opinions centered on this issue of "decolonialization," as it is sometimes called.

However, having drawn passing attention to this more recent dynamic phase of UN activity, it cannot be denied that, only when peoples and nations have exercised their right to self-determination, can the other rights and freedoms (in the words of Article 29) "be fully realized."

But one further stage has to be attained, before the full stature of freedom can be realized. Article 29 begins: "Everyone has duties to the community," and, later on it says that everyone shall be subject to the "due recognition and respect for the rights and freedoms of others and of meeting the just requirements of morality." No rights or freedoms can ever be absolute. They must be interpreted in terms of law, morality, public order, the general welfare, and the rights of others. So here is the other side of the coin: rights must be balanced by duties.

At the beginning of this pamphlet, occurred the following statement:

> "One man's right is another man's obligation. There are duties which he owes to his fellow men and duties which he expects his fellow men to have towards him. Because he is a human being, he has human rights which he shares with all his fellows."

We can repeat at the end of our study of the Declaration the point which was made then: "For this is the only way in which society can live together."

There is the Declaration in a nutshell. In the last resort, it is not the State, the government, the collectivity, which counts. It is the individual. He is the fountainhead of the constant stream of "human rights". With him and all his fellows is deposited the primary safeguarding of "the general welfare in a democratic society."

DISCUSSION SUGGESTIONS

1. "Everyone has duties to the community"—what duties? What do you consider are the essential duties of the individual to the "international order"?

2. What is the "welfare state"? How can the rights of the individual be protected when, for example, the government or local authorities appropriate private land for public or general welfare purposes?

3. In what way do you think that some of the rights and freedoms of the Declaration could be misinterpreted or misapplied, "contrary to the purposes and principles of the United Nations"?

CHAPTER VIII

What Remains To Be Done?

The perspective gained from the foregoing survey should give force to the remark made by the Chairman of the Committee working on the draft Covenants on Human Rights, when he declared:

> "This Committee has been engaged in a revolutionary effort to lay down a suitable philosophical and juridical groundwork for the new world order. Its members may well be regarded as the Encyclopedists of the Atomic Age."

If that perspective is kept before us—i.e. that the task is immense, unending, and revolutionary, in a world-wide sense—then the concerned citizen is fortified against the pessimism which might otherwise overwhelm him when the high ideals of the Declaration are set against the actual situation in the world around him. As we have seen, the *implementation* of the Declaration is still far from accomplishment. A practical answer to the question at the head of this chapter might almost be the single word: "Everything!"

CONSTITUTIONAL GUARANTEES

Nevertheless, perhaps one of the most significant developments in human rights is the fact that almost all the constitutions or basic laws of states adopted in recent years contain provisions relating to human rights and fundamental freedoms. For many of these "new" countries, the Universal Declaration of Human Rights has served as a model. At least this fact is a promise of better things, since the developing countries *start* with the Declaration as part of their fundamental law.[1]

---

[1] Countries which have incorporated certain articles of the Universal Declaration of Human Rights into their Constitutions are: Haiti (1950), Libya (1951), Eritrea (1952), The Ivory Coast, Dahomey, Gabon, Guinea, Madagascar, Senegal, Mali—all in 1958-59—, and Somalia (1960).

As noted earlier in the booklet, during the first ten years of the existence of the United Nations, the human rights program was directed primarily toward the definition of principles and the embodying of them in a series of international instruments, including the two draft Covenants described earlier, and also various other Conventions and Declarations. Since 1955, however, there has been a series of important new directions for the program. The present UN program has three main parts, namely, reports on human rights, studies of specific rights, and advisory services. Every three years member states report to the Secretary-General on the progress achieved and difficulties encountered in their respective countries. In a recent series, reports were received from 66 governments. This committee reports to the Commission on Human Rights, so a close check is kept by the UN on progress made or not made.

The second part of this operational program is a series of global studies of particular rights. These studies stress general developments, progress achieved and measures taken to safeguard human liberty and contain objective recommendations. Sources drawn upon for preparing the studies consist not only official information transmitted by governments, but also from certain non-governmental organisations and the writings of recognized scholars.

Another recent development in the human rights program was the establishment of advisory services. Services are rendered, at the request of governments, on any human rights subject, provided it is not one for which assistance is already available through technical assistance programs. Seminars are organized to bring key people together for short periods to stimulate greater awareness of these problems within "official" circles.

Moreover, an increasing number of "fellowships" are being created under the advisory program. Some examples of how the fellowship program operates may indicate its value. A Nigerian lawyer, awarded a fellowship under the 1962 program, is studying the problems of protecting human rights in the administration of criminal justice, by spending about four months in Dublin, under the supervision of the Attorney-General of Ireland, and by making an intensive study of the Irish system of criminal justice. Two high officials from Greece and Indonesia are similarly studying New Zealand's social security system. An official of the Israel Ministry of Social Welfare is now in the United States to study methods of protecting human rights through social welfare legislation. A young woman official from the Japanese Ministry of Justice is in Canada, studying ways and means of protecting human rights in criminal procedure, with particular reference to systems of parole.

FREEDOM OF MOVEMENT

At the same time, the work of the Human Rights Commission and its subsidiary bodies goes ahead. In recent years the Sub-Commission on the Prevention of Discrimination and the Protection of Minorities has been studying concrete aspects of discrimination in various walks of life, such as discrimination in education, in employment, in the matter of religious rights, in political rights, and discrimination in respect of the right of everyone to leave any country, including his own, and to return to his country. (See Article 13). In the last connection, a vast amount of new information has been brought to light by these investigations and forms the basis of a possible draft covenant or treaty in the near future. Information received from nearly 90 countries showed that the right to leave any country was by no means generally recognized as a constitutional or a legal right. In fact, only about one-third of the countries studied recognized the right. The study pointed out, however, that the formal recognition of the right "is not enough to ensure its enjoyment", nor does the *absence* of a legal recognition of the right "necessarily negate its existence."

Incidentally, the fact that this "freedom of movement" is important to *both* countries concerned was pointed out by a trade union spokesman when he called the Sub-Commission's attention to the tremendous role which the right to leave a country had played in the advancement of the under-privileged classes and, especially, of workers. Mass immigration of workers had helped to relieve the hardship to which they were exposed in their homeland, and to build up industries and trade unions in the countries to which they had come. Many of these immigrants eventually returned to their original countries, taking back with them the skills and knowledge acquired abroad, and thus con-

44

tributed appreciably to the economic and social development of their own country. This flow of labour exerted considerable influence in the cultural sphere and so assisted in strengthening means of international co-operation.

PEACE AND FREEDOM

Our last chapter concluded with the supremacy of the individual, as the source of all human rights. Yet, such is the nature of our Atomic Age that the threat of nuclear war is equally a threat to the Universal Declaration of Human Rights. For the psychological conditions which make for war are just the conditions which destroy the liberty of the individual. Peace and freedom live together or die together.

Therefore, the underlying problem of human rights is: "How to prevent War? How to create Peace"? For this reason, the *whole* apparatus of the United Nations is concerned with the protection of Human Rights. Effective disarmament, the peaceful settlement of disputes, the co-operation of nations to help each other to succeed and prosper—all these actions decrease tensions and help build alternative mechanisms to war.

The United Nations, and indeed each one of its Member-States, are committed to the new way of life proclaimed in the Declaration. It's no longer a question of remaining where we are. For the forces of world conflict will not let us stand still. We must feed the dog, or the eagle.

Since the Universal Declaration of Human Rights stands or falls by its belief in the individual and the family as the only true units of the world community, no individual or a family can contract out of that obligation without loss to mankind.

As John Donne expressed it, three centuries ago: "No Man is an Island, but Part of the Main."

CELEBRATING HUMAN RIGHTS DAY

The celebration of Human Rights Day, on 10 December each year (the anniversary of the Declaration's signature in 1948) has become increasingly widespread in countries throughout the world. These observances provide a special opportunity to focus attention on the principles set forth in the Declaration and on the need for renewed effort to promote their universal acceptance and practice in everyday life.

Careful planning and a wide range of action are involved in the celebration of Human Rights Day. At the international level, the President of the General Assembly, the Secretary-General of the United Nations and the Directors-General of the various specialized agencies issue special messages, which are widely disseminated in many languages by the different communications media. By tradition, a musical concert of outstanding quality is held at United Nations Headquarters, which is broadcast and televised to many parts of the world. The United Nations and several of the specialized agencies, particularly UNESCO, prepare and issue relevant leaflets, booklets and other publications and also special information programmes, such as radio broadcasts, photo display sets, filmstrips and other visual aids. Most of these materials are available directly from the issuing agencies and also through the United Nations Information Centres maintained at more than fifty locations in Member States throughout the world.

Within the various countries, many Governments proclaim 10 December as Human Rights Day. Special messages usually are issued by the Heads of State and sometimes also by other appropriate officials at the provincial, state and local levels. In many countries, education authorities further issue special instructions or suggestions and teaching materials to schools. New printings and translations of the Declaration are made and widely distributed in some countries, sometimes accompanied by the text of the national Bill of Rights or other documents of historic significance to the country in the efforts of its people to achieve human rights and fundamental freedom. To call general public attention to Human Rights Day, some Governments issue special postage stamps, first-day covers or special postage cancellations. In some countries, special honours or awards are presented with appropriate ceremonies to individuals, organizations or institutions that have made outstanding contributions to the advancement of human rights.

Many non-governmental organizations such as United Nations Associations, trade unions, church bodies, academic or professional associations, youth groups and the like, hold conferences, seminars or discussion groups to study current problems in the field of human rights and organize community projects or other appropriate action programmes to work on the many continuing and concrete tasks involved in promoting effective recognition and observance of the principles enunciated in the Universal Declaration.

In some countries the mass media play an active role in Human Rights Day celebrations. Newspapers sometimes reproduce the text of the Declaration, print editorials on Human Rights, provide full reports on celebration ceremonies interest to their readers. Film showings, live theatre performances or concerts may be held, often under the sponsorship of one or more community organizations as a fund-raising device for a particular human rights cause. Radio and televisions stations may use Human Rights Day spot announcements, broadcast special UN or UNESCO documentaries or features or originate their own programs on Human Rights themes.

Whatever their form, these many Human Rights Day celebrations typically emphasized the basic concept that human rights, to be meaningful, must be respected and enjoyed—not as philosophical abstractions, but concretely by all people in their everyday lives.

HOW EDUCATIONAL INSTITUTIONS CAN HELP

The crucial importance of education in the study and practice of human rights can scarcely be over-emphasized, for at least two reasons. First, real improvement in human relations and inter-group understanding usually involves basic attitude changes, which tend to take place only over a period of time and as a result of increased knowledge and perception. Schools which wish to do so can provide many opportunities for such growth. Secondly, the school constitutes to a considerable extent a community in microcosm, within which human rights can be both studied and practiced, not only on Human Rights Day but continually throughout the year.

In elementary and secondary schools, direct teaching of the Universal Declaration of Human Rights, and of other relevant documents, such as the Declaration of the Rights of the Child, may be undertaken, usually in the context of the teaching of history or the social studies. In this connexion, teachers in many countries have used the approach of having their pupils study the meaning of the articles of the Declaration against the background of the country's own struggles to achieve the rights and freedoms which the Declaration proclaims.

In a number of countries, children have themselves prepared simplified versions of the Declaration, written in their own words. Several of these versions have been published and widely distributed.

Some school classes have taken the approach of concentrating their study around a particular right, or group of related rights, considered to be of special importance within the locality, the country or the world community. Examples of such special topics include the rights of women, child labor, the right to vote, and the right to education.

As the climax of such study programmes, special school assemblies are often held on Human Rights Day, with pupils presenting the results of their deepened insights in the form of a panel discussion, a pageant, or a series of selected readings. Sometimes at such school assemblies, the featured attraction is an address by a community leader or other eminent personality who has made an outstanding contribution in the human rights field.

It may be noted that reports of actual school study programmes on human rights subjects undertaken in various parts of the world, written in the words of the teachers themselves, have been assembled by the United Nations and UNESCO.[1]

At the college and university level, the study of law, sociology, history, politics and government are among the many subjects which offer clear opportunities for the study of human rights subjects in depth. Particularly on appropriate special occasions, such as Human Rights Day, institutions of higher education might help to deepen public understanding of problems and issues in the field of human rights through presenting open lectures and symposia by members of the faculty, holding student assemblies or university-wide ceremonies, sponsoring student debates or essay, art or drama contests on human rights themes, or publishing special articles in university or professional journals.

---

[1] Published in a booklet entitled *Teaching Human Rights* (New York, United Nations, 1959, 87 pp.). A new edition of this handbook is currently in preparation and will be published by the United Nations in the autumn of 1963.

But in this field knowledge alone is not enough. As Mrs. Eleanor Roosevelt once stated "In every land, the people must accept and respect these rights and freedoms in their own communities and in their own lives, and by so doing, create countries, and in time, a world where such freedoms are a reality."[1]

DISCUSSION SUGGESTIONS

1. In what ways are war preparations an obstacle to human rights? In what ways can you constructively contribute to your government's foreign policy, and in coming to agreements with other countries?

2. Make suggestions for the celebration next Human Rights Day (10 December) in your own district, community, or organisation. What can schools do to spread knowledge about Human Rights? What corporate participation can be organised in a school known to you for arousing student interest?

3. Do you think the World Court should be permitted to entertain claims or appeals from individuals, as well as from states? What would the dangers be of such an innovation, and what the benefits?

---

[1] This statement is from a speech delivered by Mrs. Roosevelt at the first anniversary celebration of the Universal Declaration of Human Rights by the United Nations.

Part II

THE UNITED NATIONS —
WHO NEEDS IT?

CHAPTER IX

The Jobs Of The U.N.

War has always meant death, and loss; loss of life, of cultures, of resources that could not be spared. Until now, however, wars were not total. Their tragedy was awesome, but partial; that changed with the invention of thermonuclear weapons.

For the first time in history, to kill means to die; not only morally, as religious teaching has ever insisted, but now also physically. In World War III both sides would perish. There would be no victor.

To avoid total destruction—and both the U.S. and the U.S.S.R. are agreed that it should be avoided—four jobs have to be done.

—We must achieve a workable foolproof disarmament agreement.

—We must alleviate those frustrations—hunger, illiteracy and hopelessness—that have always before led to war.

—We must maintain a school for the rich, the poor, the weak and the strong to learn the new responsibilities of living together in a world where mistakes and lack of moderation can cause annihilation, and recourse to force is no longer a rational last resort.

—We must maintain machinery for keeping the great and powerful from clashing even on a small scale, because a small clash could lead to global holocaust.

These jobs must be done if we are to maintain a lasting peace. At present they are being done by various groups that operate under the name of United Nations.

DISARMAMENT

There is already a basic agreement that World War III must be avoided. In the disarmament talks that are constantly going on, mankind is trying to work out some of the details of that agreement. The talks may be compared to those that go on over a family's decision to live in a cooperative apartment building. The decision has been made but the parties are still discussing the regulations, the share of the common costs, the duties of the caretaker, the lawyer and the penalties if a tenant is unfaithful to the terms of the agreement.

The United Nations is central to these negotiations. It is a permanent peace conference, out of which pour millions of words each year. Some are agreements, some contain faint glimmers of agreement. But frequently the words seem to lead nowhere. They are the outpourings of national frustration, hungers and fears.

This is not a waste of time. For an agreement on general disarmament will prove workable only if it has taken into account both the careful calculations of the experts and the feelings, prejudices, misconceptions and frustrations of mankind.

Disarmament cannot be born in ivory towers. Its laws must be tested in a constant public brawl, where emotion will rule, side by side with caution. Otherwise, the most clever technical plans may be undone by some irrational passions that drive a nation, big or small, to violence.

ALLEVIATING FRUSTRATIONS

And it is best to hear out these passions not only for the sake of disarmament, but to help alleviate a threat as serious as the nuclear threat: the frustration of hopelessness, a national despair which could destroy world stability just as personal stress and emotion destroys mental stability in certain individuals. For most of the world's nations, the frustration of hopelessness is a daily reality.

A farmer, for instance, in a specific hungry nation has three acres, three children, a wife and a bullock. On those three acres, he raises one hundred dollars worth of crops a year. Of this, he pays the money-lender, twenty-five dollars at four percent per month. The farmer is so heavily in debt, not because he is improvident but because when one is poor as he is, it is impossible to save. The slightest misadventure—an illness, the death of the bullock—sends him, of necessity, to the money-lender. This farmer has no money in a sock under the mattress on the bed, since he does not own a sock, a mattress or a bed.

The farmer who has paid twenty-five of his yearly hundred dollars to the money-lender then pays fifteen of the remaining seventy-five to the government in taxes. So he must support himself, his wife and three children on sixteen cents a day.

They eat only cereals, grains—and just enough cereal to give a minimum diet, not a balanced diet, to one person, costs six cents per day. To feed the family at the minimum level would cost thirty cents a day—almost twice what the farmer has. The result is that the man and his wife will not be strong enough to work at their capacity. The children, if they live to grow up, will die young. This is the meaning of hopelessness for the individual. It is also the meaning of hopelessness for the nation—for this is the most wasteful, the most monstrous condition that afflicts the under-developed countries.

In richer countries, we invest eighteen years in a human being, eighteen years during which the human being grows and learns. He can then support himself, if necessary, for three times as long, for another fifty four years, into his seventies. But in a poor country, parents invest eighteen years in a human being and then he can work only eighteen years more.

It is as if one had a factory with machinery that ran down in one year instead of three. The most important piece of "machinery" in any economy, is the human machinery, and the newly developing countries are handicapped from the word "go". They have to work with "machinery" that perishes more quickly. They cannot, as a result, work as efficiently as the more developed countries. Their pace of progress is agonizingly slow and this is tragic because men are so much more than machines, and a nation is so much more than an economy.

Most of these poor countries are run by moderates. There are extremists in these countries, as in all countries—of the left and of the right—who promise to solve the problems of poverty overnight with some magical "ism". But there can be no magical overnight cure for the human condition, because the human machinery wears out too quickly, because there isn't enough capital, because there aren't enough trained men.

What men there are, of course, are desperate men who feel they have little to lose. They do not expect a better tomorrow. As a result, they are prepared to listen to the extremist. How can the moderate government of an underdeveloped country defend itself against the demagogue, who accuses the moderate leaders of pursuing an ineffectual policy subservient to richer nations?

How can the national frustration of hopelessness be eased? One way is for the moderates to shout at the rich and powerful from the U.N. podium.

A person often needs to "blow off steam," talk his frustrations out to keep himself from becoming unbalanced. Perhaps the U.N. can be viewed as a place to "blow-off-steam," not only for small nations but for big nations who sometimes also feel they have to express their frustrations, and relieve them, by speaking out.

THE U.N. AS A SCHOOL

But talking towards arriving at a disarmament treaty, or talking to relieve one's frustration is not enough. We must do something about what makes men desperate—poverty, illiteracy, disease, ignorance, backwardness, inexperience. The United Nations plays a great role in this. It plays the role of a school, one that starts at the elementary level and goes on to university standards; a school that teaches how best to use human and natural resources, and also teaches political realism.

For instance, many countries have high levels of illiteracy. One cannot build factories if there are no people to read the blueprints. One cannot have schools unless one has teachers. The United Nations through UNESCO helps set up teachers' colleges.

After the blue-prints are read and the factories are built, managers, foremen, technicians and craftsmen are needed to run them. Skilled men are very often lacking in the developing countries; so, the United Nations set up schools to train foremen and craftsmen and technicians, to work in the factories, run the textile machinery, to keep the presses and lathes running.

The farmers do not grow enough, very often because they have so little land, equally often because they do not know how to get the best out of their land. The United Nations sets up schools where instructors are trained to teach the farmers to grow better crops.

In the northwest part of India, for instance, the United Nations Special Fund, together with the Food and Agricultural Organization, will set up a training school for experts to teach Indians how to breed better sheep. The Hindu religion allows Indians to eat mutton, and yet the sheep that Indians breed, have far less meat and far less wool than the sheep in New Zealand, or

Australia, or Britain or the United States. By training experts to train herders, one can change the situation with very little money, and do something about the dangerous shortage of animal protein in the diet of the average Indian.

In all these ways, the U.N. acts as a school. The teaching reaches higher levels. One of the most expensive things a nation can do is to build "castles in Spain", or purchase "white elephants". Lack of realism is usually due to lack of experience. '

The U.N. helps with this too, by sending to many new nations, survey teams that comb the territory to discover in a very short time what resources are there. Will a certain valley be suitable as a site for a dam? What minerals exist?

It used to take up to sixty years to make such a survey. Now, by using airborne instruments, United Nations experts complete the survey in six months. The report is then presented formally to the country under survey. Such a document acquires enormous psychological strength. It gives to the people a true picture of their heritage, what they have and (just as important) what they do not have; a precise knowledge of the country's resources is the best guarantee that rash demagogues will not convince the people to try to develop what does not exist.

Once it has established what the resources are in any particular territory, the U.N. then helps the government and private entrepreneurs to establish priorities. What is more urgent, a school or a road? What should be built first? What should not be built until ten years later? There is an order—not always obvious—in which things should be done. Some things develop naturally from others. The reverse order may be wasteful. U.N. experts help people decide the proper order.

There are other aspects to the U.N.'s role of teacher. For instance, how does one organize a Ministry of Health when one never has organized such a Ministry before? The United Nations through WHO can provide experts to help train key employees. How does one run a government or administer any kind of establishment? The United Nations sets up schools for administrators where they learn the intricacies of a budget, of balancing it, proper accounting, proper personnel standards, what skills must be acquired before people can be promoted from job to job.

These are not things of which any nation is incapable but

they are things in which many nations are not trained, often because they were not given the opportunity to train.

The U.N. is not the only training school nor the only reservoir of teachers. It would be possible for any developed country to send a training mission to some under-developed country, and this is often done; but there are cases when if experts arrive from one major country, some other major country may be alarmed and ask that it too be invited to send experts. The newspapers begin to talk in terms of political competition. Country "A" accuses the experts of country "B" of being, not technicians, but spies, and vice versa. In such cases, some small nations find it safer to ask for help from the U.N.

However, the teaching does not end there. In the U.N., new nations learn the sort of realism that new legislators learn when they are first elected to their assemblies. Some of these new legislators win at the polls through their oratory and they believe that when they reach the seat of government they will change the shape of the world with their golden words. . . . It does not take them long to discover that there are committee chairmen, senior legislators, who are not easily swayed by oratory, who may not come on the floor to listen; and the new member discovers that to get along, to achieve results, he must learn to cooperate— he must learn to reach some accommodation with other members in his legislature. This is the process of politics.

In any society of any size, if human beings or human communities are to live together in one entity, they must make concessions one to the other. Nobody can have it all his own way. It is a custom, often, to treat such mutual concessions with contempt, to label them "horse-trading", to consider them as something not quite honest. And yet, the whole process of living together is compounded of such concessions, even in the elementary unit of a marriage: the partners learn not to do things that displease the other. As this is true of the individual, so it is true of town and nations.

Today, when war is no longer a rational extension of diplomacy, when power rivalries can no longer be expressed or fought out in military terms, new techniques for resolving disputes have to be devised. The search for these new techniques goes on in the U.N. The great and powerful have to woo the small and the weak, or at least hear them out, to listen to their anger and their desperation and their frustrations. And the small have to learn that mere anger will not convince the rich and powerful to share their wealth and strength.

They learn to live together—the big and the small. They learn to meet in corridors and lobbies and engage in the true, tested process of accommodation that is the essence of all peaceable political life. They learn to "horse-trade", which is much better than fighting. This is an enormously valuable lesson that is currently being taught at the U.N.

PREVENTING GREAT POWER CLASHES

Then there are the crises. Occasionally, as we seek some agreement on how not to blow ourselves up, chaos breaks out, order collapses and somewhere there is a vacuum. In the days before thermonuclear weapons, one great power or another would send a gun-boat up the river to "pacify the natives." This no longer is possible, because a rival great power may also send an expeditionary force and its gun-boats may carry nuclear weapons.

Sometimes, therefore, it is imperative not to solve crises through the traditional means of exerting national power or of exerting the power of one alliance in a certain situation. Sometimes it is better to keep the big power blocs from faicng one another in yet another arena, in yet another new crisis. But if the power of any one nation is not to be injected into a given vacuum, if those who have the military force, are not to settle situations of chaos, who will? Occasionally, the U.N. is sent, as in the Congo.

In the Congo,the United Nations has had to deal with a mess. But the United Nations went there precisely because there was a mess. If an international force had not gone to the Congo, the mess would have been worse.

Without the United Nations there would today be a primitive, tribal version of the Spanish Civil War in the Congo, with the big powers involved. And such a small war could start the big one. There will be other messes and to some of these the United Nations will have to be sent, so as not to involve the great powers. These will not be neat, tidy operations, but for so long as they prevent direct big-power rivalry, either economic or military, peace will have been served.

Thus to recapitulate, there are four roles for the U.N.

—as the world's permanent peace conference, a peace conference held in the eye of the hurricane of human emotions

—as the place where the world can "blow-off-steam"

—as a school in which we learn to live together and

—as a trouble-shooter in "messes."

HOW WELL HAS THE U.N. PERFORMED ITS FOUR JOBS?

These are being carried out, currently, by the national delegates and by a group of international civil servants sometimes known as the United Nations' family. These international civil servants are not always infallible people. They are not supermen. They are no different from the employees of other organizations, national or international. They do not have a secret formula to solve the world's problems. They are, in some instances, effective; in others, paralyzed; in certain situations, they may lack knowledge.

No one in the Secretariat had a clear idea before the Congo crisis started, of what precisely would follow. No one was really prepared for the situation. But then no one was quite prepared for such a situation anywhere in the world. There will almost certainly be other crises for which the U.N. will not be prepared and yet it will still have to take action because it will be ordered to do so. It will appear at times to flounder, at times to be making mistakes.

And people will fear such mistakes set a "precedent". Frequently, the question is asked whether there is not some way to ensure that any particular U.N. action will not be a precedent for similar actions. These are futile attempts to foreclose the future. Anything one does throughout the day is a precedent for tomorrow, but precedents work two ways: there are precedents for what to do and precedents for what not to do. The U.N., like other human organisations, has learned by its mistakes—no more, no less than other organisations learn. It tries not to repeat its mistakes—sometimes it makes new ones.

So the U.N. is something short of the miracle that its greatest admirers expected in the euphoria that followed peace in Europe and in Japan. And to some it smacks of defeatism to confess that the United Nations has all the weaknesses of other organisations; yet these very weaknesses may be the U.N.'s greatest strength.

60

If it were stronger and more efficient, it would be going, inevitably, against the reality of today, where nationalism is still a major force.

WORLD GOVERNMENT?

What of the future? Where does this all lead? Are we trying to make the U.N. evolve into a world government, running everyone's affairs, directing human activity throughout the earth? The answer is no; the U.N. is not set up to be a world government. It is, rather, like an apartment building. In each apartment one nation lives. The apartment dwellers agree that the building should not burn down, and are striving to compile a set of fire regulations to keep the edifice standing. The fire regulations do not tell people how to dress, where to worship, what to study, what jobs they may take, what to eat or how to carry on their private relations. The fire regulations help only in preventing fire.

There is a caretaker. He has no authority to break into anybody's apartment to enforce the fire regulations. He cannot tell people how to behave, or where to work. He can only sound the alarm in case of fire. He can give advice when asked. The caretaker is the U.N. civil service; the tenants are the U.N. members.

If fire breaks out in one apartment, and flames can be seen under the door, then the tenants, acting in concert, must have the right to break that door down and go in; this right belongs, not to the caretaker, but to the tenants acting in concert. They will act in concert only if there is danger of the fire spreading to their own apartments. They will not necessarily act in concert for any threat less than general conflagration.

What guarantee is there that they will act at all, even in the face of grave danger? What guarantee is there that most of the tenants in this apartment building that our world is, will try to keep it from burning down? Who will enforce the fire regulations?

Fear is the guarantee of action; fear is the great enforcer, and main stimulus towards agreement on fire regulations.

CHAPTER X

The Charter

THE MEANING OF THE CHARTER

This mythical apartment house is not unlike the structure built under the U.N. Charter. The Charter states that the purpose of the organization primarily is to "save succeeding generations from the scourge of war." But the procedures laid down for doing so are carefully calculated to prevent the U.N. from becoming a world government.

Coercive action by the direct use of force against a member who refuses U.N. intervention can be taken only if the Security Council decides to act because it finds that there is an actual threat to international peace. But such a finding can be made only if the five permanent members (Britain, China, France, the U.S.S.R. and the U.S.) agree. That is the procedure laid down in Chapter 7 of the Charter, the only chapter which binds members to obey the directives of the Security Council. In substance this means that the Russians and Americans must agree that a certain situation threatens them both before direct force can be used against a Nation which does not want U.N. intervention.

Presumably if a situation threatens only one superpower, then the other might not be prepared to initiate coercive U.N. action to redress that situation. This means that in effect the U.N. is powerless to coerce one of the two superpowers; it would be unrealistic and preposterous for the Charter to suggest otherwise since, in fact, only one of the two superpowers can coerce the other.

But if we assume, as we must assume, that both Russia and the U.S. want to prevent the war that would doom them both, then we must assume that they will prevent U.N. action only in situations that they know will not ultimately cause a world war— in situations over which they have some control.

To return to our comparison with the cooperative apartment building: among its tenants are two who are very rich and occupy the most space. Nothing can be done if these two do not concur. If a small fire in a lesser apartment does not threaten the whole building but bothers one of the two major tenants, the other major tenant may veto concerted action. He would not veto concerted action, however, if the fire were likely to get so out of control that the whole building would burn down; this we must assume. To assume otherwise is to assume that one of the major powers has become so irrational that it wants to commit suicide. Through discussions on disarmament, there is the hope that something international might be done eventually to reduce the danger of an irrational act. Meanwhile, we must not forget that the two superpowers have each taken stringent measures to see that an insane act, even on the part of their most powerful men, will not destroy them and the rest of the world.

One final point must be made on this question of coercing a superpower. Since only the other superpower could do the coercing, such coercing would lead to world war. Therefore, any who advocate that a superpower should be coerced, advocate that the two superpowers, should fight one another in a war that would destroy at least the Northern Hemisphere.

The coercive provisions of the U.N. Charter have never been used, either because they would have involved an attempt to coerce a superpower, or because less drastic measures were found sufficient.

These include the well known "Uniting for Peace" resolution under which the General Assembly can *recommend* that its members take direct collective military action when there is a breach of peace or an actual act of aggression threatening international peace. The key word is *recommend*. A recommendation is not binding as would be a directive by the Security Council under the procedures of Chapter 7.

Again, it would be absurd to suppose that the members of the General Assembly would recommend that direct military action be taken against one of the two superpowers. Only the other superpower could take such military action and the result would be world war. And it should be obvious that if either superpower decides to launch a world war, it will not wait for permission from the General Assembly. It should also be obvious that the members of the General Assembly will not vote for a world war—which is what they would be voting for if they voted for direct military action by one superpower against the other.

Short of direct physical force, the Security Council can dictate other coercive measures, such as severing commercial or diplomatic relations, demonstration, blockade, partial or total interruption of communications. Yet it is important to remember that before any policy of coercion can be considered binding on the members of the U.N., it has to be adopted unanimously by Britain, China, France, the Soviet Union and the U.S., the five permanent members of the Security Council.

In the Congo, as in the Gaza Strip, New Guinea and Korea, a U.N. military force entered at the invitation of the legal governments concerned and thus no coercion of a U.N. member was involved.

There is a whole range of services—including restoration of law and order—that the U.N. can provide if invited to do so by a nation that desires these services. However, such actions must be authorized by the Security Council or the General Assembly, as appropriate. In other words, the Secretary General can help a country in many ways on two conditions: 1) that he be asked for help by that country; 2) that he be authorized by the Security Council or the General Assembly. Both conditions must be fulfilled before he can act.

Before coercion through physical force or sanctions is applied, the U.N. is bound to try other techniques such as negotiation, enquiry, mediation, conciliation, arbitration, judicial settlements, resort to regional arrangements or other peaceful means, including quiet diplomacy by the Secretary General.

Much of this amounts to moral pressure, and a very potent weapon it is today when thermonuclear weapons have restricted freedom of action for militarily powerful nations, forcing them to compete with economic and propaganda means for the sympathy or support of smaller nations.

MAJORITIES AND BLOCS

The smaller nations, naturally try to use the thermonuclear stalemate to their own advantage and consequently are accused of playing one power bloc against another. But there is a limit to how far the small powers can go in pushing a bigger power in the U.N.; there is a limit to how much they can use the U.N. for these ends. Ultimately, the big powers with their Security

Council veto and with their wealth—they pay most of the costs—determine what the U.N. will or will not do.

The fact that the small powers try to use their votes to their own advantage has been called blackmail. If it were blackmail, it would go on, whether the U.N. existed or not, and it might be an uglier form of blackmail outside the U.N. For the U.N. has certain rules on what can be done, and how, all of which force the small nations to seek compromises.

There is no real Afroasian block. The Afroasian nations each have different objectives, often conflicting. They need different things from the big powers. As a result, when they agree on a course of action, it is usually a less extreme course than that advocated by the more militant members. In that sense, the U.N. benefits world order.

For instance, as the *Economist* of January 6, 1962 pointed out:

> The resolution of the General Assembly calling for a rapid end to colonialism was carried, on November 27th, by 97 votes to none, with the support of the older Commonwealth countries, the United States, and twelve west European countries; Britain, France, South Africa and Spain abstained. Russia withdrew a much (stronger) draft, on finding that the Asian and African members in fact would not back it. The resolution condemning South Africa's racialist policies, and urging it to change them, was carried by 97 to 2, with the support of every west European country except Portugal. Another draft, mainly backed by African states, and envisaging sanctions against South Africa, failed to get through—largely because India and a dozen other Asians would not back it. Of the two main resolutions on South West Africa, one was carried without a division; the other by 90 to 1 (Portugal), Belgium, Britain, France and Spain abstaining. The resolution condemning Portugal's failure to comply with its UN obligations on colonies was carried by 90 to 3 (Portugal, South Africa and Spain), France and Bolivia abstaining. The Arabs put up a moderate resolution on Algeria, which was carried without opposition, and (a stronger) one on Oman, which failed to collect even half of the Afro-Asian votes.

So we see that the small powers will not vote to coerce a superpower, since this would mean war between the superpowers. Then there are limits, inherent in the character of the U.N. itself, to how much the small powers can use their votes to put pressure, short of physical force, on the bigger powers.

Yet even people who ought to know better speak of the dangers to the bigger powers, posed by the "irresponsibility" of the small nation majority in the U.N.

This accusation of "irresponsibility" is based mainly on the impatience of the Afroasians with continued colonial domination and with any form of racial discrimination—the only issues on which one can detect some form of Afroasian bloc. Emotionally, the attitude of the new nations is understandable. They have suffered racial slights even in their own countries, and because of their colour, were denied certain privileges enjoyed by their white masters.

They have also known foreign domination which not infrequently denied them the chance of self-improvement. They are therefore naturally skeptical of pleas for postponement of independence. Yet where the pleas of postponement have been accompanied by a reasonably trustworthy promise of progress toward independence, the Afroasians have been cooperative. Britain has felt very little pressure from the Afroasians in her efforts to transform her colonial empire into a commonwealth of independent nations.

But where ultimate independence is denied, the manhood of the subject nation and of the whole race is denied. This is hard to accept.

The demands for complete and immediate end to colonialism and racialism, and for pressures to accomplish this aim, are said to be against the principles of the U.N. Charter which, according to some, laid the whole emphasis on the organization of peace through collective security—expecting that the great powers would deal in concert with any breach of the peace by the smaller powers.

Discussing this issue, the *Economist* wrote on January 6, 1962 that such criticism of the U.N.

> suggests a nineteenth-century nostalgia for the brave old world in which the great powers kept (or supposedly kept) the pax Metternichiana. But there is more in the founding fathers' Charter than one might suppose from (the critics') selective emphasis on law and order and the primacy of the great powers. Mr. Hammarsjköld, in the introduction of his last annual report—a polical testament which all foreign ministers might profit by reading—pointed out, as one of the UN's fundamentals, the fact that the 51 founding govern-

ments asserted "the equal rights . . . of nations large and small." Their stated purposes, moreover, included the furthering of self-determination for all peoples. Those members that were colonial powers promised "to take due account of the political aspirations of the peoples" of their dependencies, and to help them to develop "free political institutions". It would be charitable to suppose that lack of acquaintance with these Charter provisions accounts for . . . flat statements, attributing (troubles in former colonies) simply to the "premature grant of independence to a country whose people were totally unprepared." Such a statement implies that the colonial power's only fault was granting independence too soon; it contains no breath of criticism of that power's neglect of its promise to take account of the dependent people's aspirations and to help them build their own political institutions. . . .

The preamble to the Charter announces a determination "to ensure, by the acceptance of principles *and the institution of methods,* that armed force shall not be used, save in the common interest" (our italics). It has never been seriously argued that the aim of this outlawing of war was to perpetuate the status quo of 1945. Any such argument would not only be absurd in itself; it would also flatly conflict with much else that the Charter contains, and which implies a world of substantial change, particularly in colonial matters.

Here lies the most durable of the dilemmas of the United Nations. And, without doubt, it is a very real dilemma. A century ago, when Italy won its national unity, its struggle was supported by liberal opinion everywhere. . . Is the UN Charter to be so construed that, if it had applied at the time of the Risorgimento, (the Italian fight for independence) the organisation would have been bound to condemn Cavour, Garibaldi and Napoleon III, and to uphold Austrian, Neapolitan and papal authority? Neither the letter of the Charter, nor the known intentions of the UN's founders, supports such a construction in favour of the petrification of the status quo. On the other hand, it is quite certainly the UN's clear purpose to prevent international violence, or failing that to restrict it. To approve the use of armed force to achieve national aspirations would be to open Pandora's box; the nations have signally failed to find an agreed definition of aggression, and could not possibly find one that distinguished aspirations justifying the use of force from aspirations that did not justify it. Any attempt to do so would be perilous indeed.

Between the two extremes of barring all violent change

in the status quo and of opening the door to a calamitous free-for-all, lies a huge void. Should it not be a major objective of all who are concerned with shaping UN decisions to seek to fill this void by "the institution of methods" that could secure a peaceful transformation of obviously explosive situations before the ultimate resort to arms occurs? Mr. Hammarskjold's concept of a UN executive capacity, clearly pointed in just this direction . . . To confine UN executive action to conciliation . . . means to leave the void aching—and thereby to make resort of violence more likely and the scale of the likely clash larger.

Discussing the search for methods to secure the peaceful transformation of obviously explosive situations, Mr. Herbert Nicholas, Fellow of New College, Oxford, wrote (*Encounter*, February 1962) that the membership of African states in the U.N., and, as a corollary, their participation in the tasks (e.g. the Congo force) of the Organization as well as the benefits (e.g. technical aid) provide the strongest guarantees that their "non-alignment" will not end in their being swept into extremism. It is useless to allege—or indeed to deny—wrote Mr. Nicholas, that the Afroasians introduce elements of unpredictability, uncertainty, irresponsibility, and even, on occasion, sheer incomprehension, into the working of the U.N. This is because these elements exist in the real world to which we and they belong. To try to exclude them from the U.N. would be like trying to preserve a neat and cosy model at the price of distorting reality. In the present "twilight of colonialism", Mr. Nicholas continued, we are not going to see the independent states of Africa line up behind the leadership of a European Great Power as the Latin Americans did behind the United States. The one chance there is of retaining their support for some sort of orderly and peaceful development in international relations, rather than see them seduced by extremism or relapse into anarchy, lies in the leadership of a U.N. Secretary-General they can trust—though of course, he in turn will need all the support the great powers can give him.

The issue, said Professor Nicholas, is repeatedly presented in terms of an impossible "either-or"—of an ideally enlightened, evolutionary and pacific policy such as a colonialist power operating the most altruistic form of trusteeship might conceivably aspire to (but has in fact never sustained long), versus a muddled, incompetent, ill-informed, inexperienced, partisan and polyglot U.N. operation. With an astonishing indifference to the West's true interests, the real alternatives are persistently ignored said Mr. Nicholas. The alternatives are quite simply either a U.N. sponsored policy, necessarily largely Afro-Asian manned, and openly aimed at fostering African nationalism and independence, or a free-for-all which would allow extremist developments on a massive scale with conflict developing rapidly from civil strife to inter-African war and finally to inter-continental war.

AREAS AND MEANS OF U.N. ACTION

The course Mr. Nicholas favours is not a formula for dealing with every crisis. And indeed there are many situations in which U.N. cannot act. But to argue that since the U.N. cannot help in every situation, it should not help in any, is to argue that one should not bother to immunize against smallpox because there is no vaccine against cancer. Surveying the record of the U.N., Mr. Nicholas continued:

> If one looks back over the areas of conflict in which the U.N. has intervened since Korea it is apparent that none of them is at the centre of the East-West cold war.
>
> Wisely, the U.N., and particularly the Secretary-General, has not attempted to insert itself into the direct confrontation of the two rival blocs, of N.A.T.O and the Warsaw Pact. It has not aspired to control summit meetings or to settle Berlin—or even Quemoy and Matsu. The areas in which it has operated, with varying success, have been those on the fringe of the main wrestling match, where other elements contribute to the local conflicts and the Great Powers, though involved, do not feel that every gain or set-back is, for them, a direct matter of life or death. The Middle East, *par excellence*, has been such a U.N. area. Africa, almost to the same degree. Much of Asia, especially where the conflicts, like those of India and Pakistan, have been predominantly intra-continental. The conflicts that develop in these areas hold the gravest potentialities for world peace because if they spread, the cold war will grow hot at their touch, but fortunately they do not themselves immediately involve the vital interests of the supersensitive . . . Great Powers.
>
> This is what makes possible the processes of U.N. mediation, intervention, even ultimately perhaps, as in

the Congo, (use of military force). The frozen posture of East and West which seems to inhibit all movement in the heartland of the cold war has not yet spread here. But of course, it can spread in a twinkling, as . . . rocket diplomacy over Suez, or the persistent . . . threats to offer direct aid to the Congo testify. And the menace of such intervention is far from adequately met by counter-threats —"If you intervene, we will"—since this only enthrones the evil it seeks to prevent. The only weapon at our disposal here is the U.N. And, since Great Power initiatives are suspect—not only by each side but by the "uncommitted" denizens of the areas involved, the only initiative possible is time and time again, the Secretary-General's. Whether he exercises it entirely *sua sponte* or via a delegation of authority from the Security Council or the General Assembly is consequently of little moment. The reason in each case will be the same, namely that in the present East-West deadlock, he often represents the only element of movement left and the only prospect of keeping the cold war from taking over Afro-Asia (and perhaps Latin America too). Though Congo confusion, tireless propaganda, and persistent misrepresentation have overlaid the fact, it is (the Secretary-General) we have to thank that Russian and American "volunteers" are not at this moment slugging it out in the jungles of the Congo.

. . . The U.N. Expeditionary Force in Gaza was not, of course, in any sense a policeman enforcing the law. It was a buffer between opposing fighting forces, actually assisting a bloodless Anglo-French evacuation and providing certain guarantees for property and security, as well as saving a considerable amount of face.

It was not the U.N. that made Britain and France withdraw; it was U.S. pressure. Once they had decided to withdraw, the U.N. provided the means for making this withdrawal less painful. The British, French and Israelis did not have to hand over the Suez Canal to the Egyptians—such a direct handover might have led to renewed incidents.

They handed over to the U.N. and there were certain real and implied guarantees connected with the U.N. presence that Britain and France would not be subject to pressure in the Suez Canal Zone.

Naturally, neither Britain nor France liked what happened at Suez. There may be other cases in which big powers, even superpowers, may embark on an enterprise and find that the costs of continuing it are too great. In such cases it might be easier for the major power or the superpower to retreat seemingly in deference to a U.N. resolution rather than retreat in obvious response to a military or economic threat by another power.

This means that conceivably, the U.N. may appear again and again to be the instrument which thwarts a minor or major power. But, if the major power is prepared to be thwarted in a certain enterprise, it must be inferred that the enterprise was not vital, that it was being tried out with no thought of persistence to the danger point of a military clash.

In such situations, the interested power would naturally prefer to succeed; but short of success, it would prefer to be balked by the U.N. rather than by another power. U.N. intervention is resented but not as much as intervention by a military rival.

Thus we may encounter, in the future, occasions when a major power will feel injured by a particular U.N. operation, yet will not veto this operation. The alternatives for the major power in question are not, of course, freedom of action as compared with U.N. opposition. The real alternatives are between U.N. opposition and opposition by another power, and of the two, opposition by the U.N. is safer. In this way, the U.N. provides flexibility for the cold war.

CHAPTER XI

The Meaning Of The Charter In Practice

DISARMAMENT

On this subject the U.N. has acted as the moral conscience of the world. It has consistently pressed for measures to end the arms race, reduce the dangers of war and end the poisoning of the atmosphere with fallout from nuclear tests.

Naturally, the primary role in disarmament negotiations belongs to the great powers; but the overall U.N. membership has kept up a steady demand that these negotiations continue. Russia and America both have solemnly declared, before the U.N. that they favour general and complete disarmament. Many differences have been eliminated. Though there is no agreement, the positions are much closer.

All discussions on disarmament since 1946 have sought agreement on foolproof methods of control which could satisfy all parties concerned. No disarmament plan proposes that foolproof control should be exercised by the United Nations Security Council, the Military Staff Committee, the Under-Secretary for Political and Security Affairs or any other existing U.N. instrumentality. Specific control mechanism will have to be designed for the sole purpose of implementing and supervising a disarmament agreement.

The United Nations has .the authority under its Charter to create foolproof control mechanisms for a disarmament agreement. Article 7, paragraph 2, of the Charter states that such organs as may be found necessary may be established in accordance with the present Charter. It is obvious that any new organ established for the express purpose of disarmament control must satisfy the national security needs of all nuclear powers before any one nuclear power will agree to disarm.

TROUBLE-SHOOTING

By a Security Council resolution, the U.N. launched its operation in the Congo at the express request of the legal

Congolese Government after the country collapsed into total chaos in July 1960. (The Katanga Province, as a whole, was no more free of chaos than other provinces.)

The Security Council resolution to send a U.N. force into the Congo was taken without a dissenting vote (July 14, 1960). This decision was reaffirmed by the Security Council again and again (July 22, 1960, August 9, 1960, February 21, 1961, November 24, 1961). The International Court of Justice upheld the legality of the Secretary-General's mandate to act as he did in the Congo. The U.N., moreover, took various actions in the Congo only at the request of the legal Congolese government.

In May 1960, the Belgians organized the only elections ever held in the Congo. In Katanga Province, Mr. Tshombe's party, the Conakat (the political arm of the Lunda and Bayeke tribes which support him) won 91,116 votes. The Conakat stood for secession. The Balubakat party which opposed secession received 134,916 votes. Mr. Tshombe lost in his own capital city of Elisabethville. In fact, considerably more than half of Katanga's population belong to the tribal elements opposing the tribes behind Tshombe.

Even so, did not this minority government have the right of revolution? Not if their revolution meant they would commit genocide on the Katangese majority opposed to Mr. Tshombe's revolution.

Mr. Tshombe's soldiers—all from his own tribe—did not choose peaceful political means to impose their pro-secessionist policy. Charles Griffith, one of Tshombe's foreign soldiers, speaking over the British Broadcasting Corporation, told of orders he had to kill all Balubas—the tribe opposed to secession. Mr. Griffith was asked by the BBC interviewer if men, women and children were covered by his orders. He replied: "Our instructions were, 'Shoot the lot; if you can't shoot them, starve them'."

As a result of such treatment, the majority of the Katangese population opposed to secession was in grave danger. They had tribal allies in other parts of the Congo, and such are tribal loyalties, that they alone would have made inevitable a war between Tshombe and the rest of the Congo. Tshombe obtained foreign military supplies and personnel for his side.

If the U.N. had not been there, Tshombe's opponents would

73

have sought outside military aid also. There was a clear danger of the Congo's becoming an international battleground.

To prevent civil war and genocide, the U.N. needed freedom of movement throughout the Congo, including Katanga where Mr. Tshombe's forces were massacring the Balubas. Fighting broke out only when Mr. Tshombe's foreign soldiers attacked the U.N. force with the express purpose of making its presence in Katanga impossible. From December 24, 1962 until December 28, 1962, U.N. troops were subject to constant fire. A U.N. helicopter was shot down and one of its occupants wounded. He was subsequently kicked to death by Mr. Tshombe's troops. After holding its fire for nearly a week, the U.N. was forced to act in self-defense, to clear the position from which it was being attacked.

What followed was a complete collapse of Mr. Tshombe's forces into a dangerous rabble. Civilian officials in town after town asked the U.N. to advance further to protect them from this rabble. Entering the town of Jadotville, U.N. troops shot a civilian car, wounded the driver and killed his wife and another passenger.

The heartrending photograph of the bleeding, bereaved man, rightly shook the world. There are no excuses for incidents of this kind and the explanations are inadequate. It is a fact that civilian cars had sped through U.N. troops repeatedly in the past to fling out hand-grenades. The International Red Cross protested the use of its emblem by civilian cars firing against the U.N. It is also probable that the troops which had been under repeated fire and were trying not to become targets, could not see too clearly what was inside a car that might have been another sneak attacker.

Yet these are only explanations, not excuses. Stringent measures to avoid such incidents, broke down tragically in this case and so the charges of atrocities against the U.N. were revived.

The International Press Institute has said, regarding the charges, that to accuse the U.N. of atrocities "implying the deliberate taking of civilian life was a blatant misrepresentation." And Mr. Frank Aiken, Irish Foreign Minister, has spoken of "a deliberate war of nerves and slander against the U.N.." The Representative of the International Committee of the Red

Cross repudiated a statement attributed to him in which he alledgedly condemned "U.N. atrocities".

Even so, critics complain that the U.N. set a dangerous precedent by interfering in what they consider a civil war, a purely internal matter. But the truth is that outside interference, actual and potential, was so heavy that this was hardly a matter of "civil" war when the U.N. became involved. More fundamentally, we must again consider the consequences of this thermonuclear age.

To repeat, it is no longer possible for one or another great power to impose world peace as did the Roman and British empires. No one power can undertake such a task without risking war and a thermonuclear war will have no victors—only vanquished.

The Congo is an illustration of a situation in which order breaks down, chaos occurs, vacuum is created, inviting outside interference, thus becoming a possible fuse that could blow up our world. Mankind, therefore, became obliged to seek new means of preserving international law and order. We cannot stop seeking or experimenting.

The U.N. operation in the Congo is such a quest, such an experiment. It has not been perfect; experiments seldom are, but without them there can be no discoveries and—in the political context—there can be no delivery from the fear of war.

At every stage of the Congo operation there was opposition by some U.N. members and support by others. It is significant that no power was so opposed as to withdraw from the world organization or to recognize Mr. Tshombe's attempt at secession.

However much some powers felt the operation opposed their interest in the Congo, they preferred to be opposed by the U.N. rather than by another power, and were not prepared to wreck the organization. Thus we are faced with circumstances in which U.N. members are not unanimous in support of an operation; some may like it; some may oppose it, but all wish the U.N. to continue.

FINANCING

The opposition need not be complete. It may be partial and qualified, or take the form of withholding contributions towards a particular enterprise of the organization.

Is this according to the Charter which states that the expenses of the organization shall be borne by the members? The International Court of Justice, in an advisory opinion has ruled that the costs of the United Nations operations in the Congo and the Middle East are expenses of the organization within the meaning of the Charter. The General Assembly, by a heavy margin, voted to adopt the decision of the International Court of Justice.

Article 19 of the Charter states that if a member is two full years in arrears on the payment of its assessments, it loses its vote automatically in the General Assembly.

But apart from these legal aspects of the case, there are other ways of looking at such situations.

Power "A" feels that its policy is incommoded by certain U.N. activities, and refuses to pay for them. Power "B" has to ask itself whether it really wants these U.N. activities to continue, whether it finds them truly necessary. Then Power "B" must decide whether it is in its interest to assume an extra financial burden and pay for these activities, even though Power "A" will not pay.

Not every U.N. member paid for the Korean War. It could have been fought by national forces, without any involvement of the U.N. Certain powers, the U.S. among them, felt however, that there was a role for the U.N. in this war. Other powers so resented U.N. involvement that they refused to support the Korean operation.

Yet even those powers did not withdraw from the U.N. Using the U.N. flag diluted the confrontation of the power blocs. The supporters of the operation felt that it was sufficiently in their interest to go on paying even though not every member paid.

To some this demonstrates that the spirit of the Charter, as they see it, was violated; but it also demonstrates that the existence of the U.N. adds an element of flexibility in the cold war, helps avoid the direct, ineluctable confrontations of the great. The Charter itself has proved flexible enough for a changing world.

In the case of the Congo, while the debate continued on financing, the organization was not paralysed. It displayed enough flexibility and resilience to continue its efforts and to prevent once more the direct involvement of national forces on opposite sides of a dispute.

Financing will remain a serious problem, inevitably so, since certain U.N. operations will be supported by some members and merely tolerated by others as the lesser of two evils. New devices to avoid financial crisis will be evolved, no doubt, from time to time. In New Guinea, for instance, in Yemen and in North Borneo* and Sarawak*, the formula has been for the powers most directly concerned to pay the expenses rather than have these met by the general membership.

Whatever the formula, however much the cost, the U.N., so far, has been a great bargain, even for the nation that pays most —the U.S.

The U.S. pays 32.07% of the U.N. budget and is the largest contributor roughly because contributions are assessed on the basis of ability to pay and national wealth, with a reservation that no one nation should pay above a certain percentage; (the General Assembly has gone on record saying that eventually no one member should pay more than thirty percent).

Because not everyone has paid, the U.S. has, at times, paid more than its share. Even so, the U.N. has been a bargain even for Americans, the biggest contributors. For example, it took an average of 18,000 U.N. men three years to restore some semblance of law and order to the Congo and keep the country functioning economically. This operation cost the U.S., in three years, approximately one hundred and eighty million dollars.

If U.S. troops had been used to do the job—and two American presidents, one Republican the other a Democrat agreed that the job had to be done—the cost to the U.S. would have been three times as much. It would have taken 18,000 U.S. troops three years to do it, since the Congo is more than three times the size of Texas and lacks communications. Each American soldier costs $10,000 a year to maintain in the field—that amounts to $30,000 over three years, $540 million for 18,000 troops, three times more than the U.N. operation has cost the U.S.

For all activities of the U.S. and its affiliated agencies, the U.S. in 1962 spent $235.3 million, which means that in 1962 each

---

* The U.N. was entrusted with ascertaining whether the people of those territories wanted to join Malaysia.

U.S. citizen contributed $1.27 to the U.N. Here is where the money went:

Approximately $50 million, or 27 cents per American went to the United Nations for peace keeping activities, for picking up messes, including the military operations in the Congo, the United Nations Emergency Force of 5,000 men in the Gaza Strip, the United Nations Truce Supervisory Organiaztion in the Middle East, and the peaceful transfer of West Irian from Dutch rule to Indonesian Administration.

Two United Nations programs of *development assistance* which are financed by voluntary funds received $45 million from the U.S. in 1962, the equivalent of 24 cents per U.S. citizen:

The Expanded Program of	
Technical Assistance	10 cents
The Special Fund	14 cents

Two other voluntary programs received $37 million from the U.S. in 1962, the equivalent of 19½ cents from each U.S. citizen:

UNICEF	6½ cents
United Nations Relief and Works	
Agency for Palestine Refugees	13 cents

To meet its part of the regular *assessed budgets* of the United Nations and ten of its related agencies, the U.S. contributed $46 million or 25 cents per inhabitant. They went to:

United Nations	13 cents
Food for Agriculture Organization	2½ cents
International Labour Organization	1½ cents
UNESCO	2½ cents
World Health Organization	4 cents

Five other U.N. Agencies each cost an average of 1/5 of a cent per American:

World Meteorological Organization
International Civil Aviation Organization
International Telecommunication Union
Universal Postal Union
Intergovernmental Maritime Consultative
 Organization

CHAPTER XII

The U.N. As A School

The United Nations, with the 13 cents each American contributed to its regular budget, helped to control illegal trade in narcotics, promoted industrial development, and financed the operations of regional economic commissions in Europe, Asia, Africa and Latin America. It also helped finance research on world social problems, efforts to codify international law, measures to promote arms control and international cooperation in space. The U.N. provided a unique and indispensable forum where economic, political and technical views could be exchanged and agreements negotiated.

The United Nations Expanded Program of Technical Assistance in 1962 dispatched 2,552 experts of 95 different nationalities to help 120 countries and territories. Their assistance was offered through the U.N. and its specialized agencies in such fields as agricultural production, health services, economic planning, resource exploration and development of administrative services, industrial research and production, peaceful uses of atomic energy, auxiliary services to industry and agriculture, education, public utilities, power, transport and communications, community development, fighting juvenile delinquency and other social services including housing and rehabilitation of the handicapped. At the same time, fellowships enabled 3,831 nationals of developing countries to study abroad in 1962.

UNESCO, in 1962, concentrated on assisting the low-income countries where 45 percent of the world's children are without schools. Almost 800 experts were at work in the field to help prepare teachers, build better school buildings, write improved textbooks ,and above all make workable plans for coping with the education problem on a long-range basis. Educational planning, with over 40 missions, was a keynote of the year's work; two new centres were opened in Beirut and New Delhi. UNESCO also helped its member states develop information services for their peoples. In addition, there was an intensification of international scientific research in the Indian Ocean and the South

Atlantic, as well as new cooperation in the field of earthquakes. In the cultural field, the organisation continued its efforts to save the Nubian monuments from the rising waters of the Nile.

Help, sometimes, is no help. A gift, a loan or an investment in a developing country might be largely wasted if that country does not have trained people to put to work the help they get. Even if there are trained people, they will not make the best use of the help they receive if they do not know the resources of their country, what can be developed and what cannot. Moreover, unless a developing country can show it has resources ripe for development, that country will not attract investment; businessmen—local as well as international—will not launch into the unknown with their shareholders' money.

This vital "pre-investment" work—producing technical and managerial skills, proving resources, stimulating investments—is the main business of *The United Nations Special Fund*.

The Special Fund runs surveys that reveal what wealth exists in a nation's land, water, minerals, oil, forests. The Special Fund helps set up programming units of experts who can put first things first on the priority lists of developing countries. It helps set up schools for administrators, managers, technical experts, foremen and ordinary craftsmen even. It also helps with Teachers' Colleges because without high school graduates, no country can beat poverty.

All this is essential pre-investment work. Its cost, like seed-money, is little. It yields rich and indispensible harvests.

The Special Fund is not charity. The country receiving aid nearly always matches it with more, for the project on its own soil and for projects in other less fortunate lands. Further, the Special Fund mobilizes resources from many countries all over the world.

As a result, for every dollar's worth of project completed with Special Fund participation, the United States pays only seventeen cents. Other forms of economic aid often cost the U.S. a full hundred cents to the dollar. By the end of 1962 the contribution of the United States to the Special Fund's 246 projects thus far approved reached 98 million. The total cost of these projects is 589 million and their yield is incalculable.

Every Special Fund operation is a telling lesson in the no-nonsense, no-frills, self-help approach to economic development.

The projects are being implemented by more than 800 international experts recruited through the United Nations and eight of its related organizations acting as Executing Agencies. In training alone, technical institutes and university departments assisted by the Special Fund are providing advanced training to over 4,000 engineering and technical students; industrial training centres are upgrading the skills of about 4,000 teachers, foremen and supervisors, and nearly 3,000 have completed their training. Close to 800 persons are attending courses in civil aviation schools, and specialized training is also being given in a number of other fields.

The World Health Organization in 1962 participated in 817 health projects in 143 countries and territories. It led the fight against smallpox, cholera, polio, tuberculosis, yaws, trachoma, syphilis and malaria. Disease knows no boundaries; it must be fought on an international basis. WHO also helped to train nursing personnel in 58 countries, and established a school in the Congo to train the first Congolese nurses. Almost 100 teachers in the medical field were sent to give courses in nursing institutions in 38 low-income countries. At the same time, 240 teachers of medical subjects from these countries were enabled to take advanced training abroad, most of them under the Expanded Program for Technical Assistance. Meanwhile, WHO continued to promote the use of clean water, supervised international quarantine measures and the collection of health statistics and supported health research projects.

The International Labour Organization in 1962 assisted developing countries in training manpower, drafting labour codes and improving labour and management relations. Its efforts to improve productivity ranged from development of rural industries to studies on the effects of automation, from protection of workers against industrial risks to development of handicrafts and social security laws.

The International Atomic Energy Agency provided expert assistance and equipment in such fields as the application of radio-isotopes in medicine, the establishment of health and safety measures related to the handling of atomic materials, laboratory research and instruction in physics, chemistry, medicine and biology; and the surveying and processing of uranium and other raw materials related to atomic energy.

The World Meteorological Organization assisted in developing national weather services and expanding existing ones. Its experts also contributed to national efforts to harness natural energy resources, such as solar radiation and wind power, and offered advice on new weather-observing instruments, forecasting techniques and the role of meteorology in developing water resources. Good global weather forecasting is needed by everyone and can only be developed on an international basis.

The International Civil Aviation Organization sent many technicians to work directly with national aviation officials to improve safety and economy in air operations, especially through training in air traffic control procedures, radio and aircraft operation, and maintenance and repair. For example, they helped in designing new airports, in installing ground radar and navigational beacons, in training control tower personnel and demonstrating new safety equipment. Air safety is an international problem that can have only international solutions.

The Food and Agriculture Organization of the United Nations during 1962 had some 550 technical assistance experts working in the field in over 100 countries. Its work covered such activities as raising agricultural productivity, developing new markets for fisheries and farm produce, livestock improvement, and the application of radio-isotopes to agricultural research. Final approval of the "Freedom-from-Hunger" campaign in which more than 50 countries are participating is an intensification of the whole of FAO's activities for increasing world food production and improving nutrition.

The United Nations Children's Fund (UNICEF) in 1962 extended its activities to include projects devoted to teenage education and vocational training. The addition of 20 projects of this kind brought the total number of projects to 401, covering 116 countries. The main part of the program concerned health services, nutrition and disease control centered on the family unit, with particular pre-occupation with the welfare of young children. The move into education and training was made in line with the emphasis being laid in the United Nations Development Decade on the development of the human resources of the low income countries.

The Universal Postal Union's constitution (the Universal Postal Convention) states that all members form "a single postal teritory for the reciprocal exchange of correspondence." Thus, a letter mailed in one hemisphere will be delivered safely even to a remote village halfway around the world; although it may go through post offices of a dozen countries, it will be handled in accordance with uniform procedures accepted by all UPU members. Moreover, every member has agreed to transmit that letter from abroad by the best means used for its own mail.

The Convention also, among other things, provides for the redirection or return of correspondence that cannot be delivered; regulates registered correspondence; sets up methods for making transit payments when the mail goes through the territory of several members; and guarantees freedom of transit throughout the entire territory of the Union. The Convention itself regulates international transmission of "ordinary mail". In addition, supplementary agreements set forth arrangements for eight other postal services such as insured mail, parcels and money orders.

To help governments modernize and speed up mailing procedures, UPU recently established a new Consultative Commission for Postal Studies. In investigating technical, operational and economic problems of post offices, it is seeking, for example, information on latest developments in mechanization and automation in sorting operations, automatic machines for selling stamps and other postal items, and the most efficient organizaion of postal offices. Replies will be gathered by UPU's International Bureau, or permanent secretariat, and made available to all members.

In other services to members, the International Bureau studies specific postal problems on request; operates a films and information library loan service for members; publishes general information needed by postal administrations; gives opinions on disagreements arising on postal questions; and acts as a clearing house for settling international postal accounts.

The International Telecommunication Union maintained and extended, in 1962, international cooperation for the improvement and rational use of telecommunication of all kinds.

It promoted the development of technical facilities and their most efficient operation with a view to improving the efficiency of telecommunication services, increasing their usefulness and making them, so far as possible, generally available to the public.

And it harmonized the actions of nations in the attainment of those common ends.

Doing the jobs of all these agencies of the United Nations family internationally spreads the cost till the services listed above could be had by the average American—the largest contributor—for $1.27.

Many of these are jobs that can only be performed internationally. Many are best performed internationally, if we are to avoid spreading the cold war, if we are to pass from mutual terror to a less harrowing way of avoiding war.

In performing these necessary international tasks, the U.N. and its specialized agencies are shaping a new kind of man—the international civil servant. The Charter says the Secretary General and his staff "shall not seek or receive instructions from any government or from any other authority external to the organization," and that they shall "refrain from any action which might reflect on the organization". Members of the United Nations undertake to respect "the exclusively international character of the Secretary General and the Staff and not to seek to influence them in the discharge of their responsibilities".

In the famous introduction to his last report to the General Assembly on the work of the organization, Mr. Hammarskjöld wrote:

"While it may be true that no man is neutral, in the sense that he is without opinions or ideals, it is just as true that, in spite of that, a neutral secretariat is possible. Anyone of integrity, not subjected to undue pressure, can, regardless of his own views, readily act in an exclusively international spirit and can be guided in his actions on behalf of the organization, solely by its interests and principles and by the instruction of its organs."

There have been some—a few—international civil servants who have not fitted the Hammarskjöld definition; but most have. Even if they joined unconvinced, the atmosphere of common purpose, the pressure of the job itself, imperceptibly led them to strive for the ideal spelled out by Hammarskjöld. This is so, perhaps, because the "exclusively international spirit" was the only one in which they could act together with people from other nationalities.

These international civil servants are not, on the whole, uncommon men. But they all work at the same task and these tasks have a momentum of their own. They all believe moreover, sooner or later that we all need the U.N.

These international civil servants and the member governments of the U.N. are forced to work together. They do not dare work against one another in the thermonuclear era, and the human search for a better, healthier, richer life makes international solutions unavoidable.

Out of common effort for common purposes, new habits, new techniques, new ways of thinking spring. Each time a common solution is found, the next common solution becomes a little easier.

Peace depends ultimately on trust and trust rises from experience in joint endeavour. Imperceptibly, trust is being built at the U.N. despite the dissensions.

We are learning lessons that we need to learn if we are to have the cooperation necessary for the effective policing of a disarmament agreement. This, perhaps, this common work, and the habits it engenders, may prove to be the greatest contribution of the U.N.

APPENDIX 1

UNIVERSAL DECLARATION OF HUMAN RIGHTS

Preamble

Whereas recognition of the inherent dignity and of the equal and inalienable rights of all members of the human family is the foundation of freedom, justice and peace in the world,

Whereas disregard and contempt for human rights have resulted in barbarous acts which have outraged the conscience of mankind, and the advent of a world in which human beings shall enjoy freedom of speech and belief and freedom from fear and want has been proclaimed as the highest aspiration of the common people,

Whereas it is essential, if man is not to be compelled to have recourse, as a last resort, to rebellion against tyranny and oppression, that human rights should be protected by the rule of law,

Whereas it is essential to promote the development of friendly relations between nations,

Whereas the peoples of the United Nations have in the Charter reaffirmed their faith in fundamental human rights, in the dignity and worth of the human person and in the equal rights of men and women and have determined to promote social progress and better standards of life in larger freedom,

Whereas Member States have pledged themselves to achieve, in cooperation with the United Nations, the promotion of universal respect for and observance of human rights and fundamental freedoms,

Whereas a common understanding of these rights and freedoms is of the greatest importance for the full realization of this pledge,

Now therefore

THE GENERAL ASSEMBLY proclaims

This Universal Declaration of Human Rights as a common standard of achievement for all peoples and all nations, to the end that every individual and every organ of society, keeping this Declaration constantly in mind, shall strive by teaching and education to promote respect for these rights and freedoms and by progressive measures, national and international, to secure their universal and effective recognition and observance, both among the peoples of Member States themselves and among the peoples of territories under their jurisdiction.

Article 1. All human beings are born free and equal in dignity and rights. They are endowed with reason and conscience and should act towards one another in a spirit of brotherhood.

Article 2 Everyone is entitled to all the rights and freedoms set forth in this Declaration, without distincion of any kind, such as race, colour, sex, language, religion, political or other opinion, national or social origin, property, birth or other status. Furthermore, no distinction shall be made on the basis of the political, jurisdictional or international status of the country or territory to which a person belongs, whether it be independent, trust, non-self-governing or under any other limitation of sovereignty.

Article 3. Everyone has the right to life, liberty and security of person.

Article 4. No one shall be held in slavery or servitude; slavery and the slave trade shall be prohibited in all their forms.

Article 5. No one shall be subjected to torture or to cruel, inhuman or degrading treatment or punishment.

Article 6. Everyone has the right to recognition everywhere as a person before the law.

Article 7. All are equal before the law and are entitled without any discrimination to equal protection of the law. All are entitled to equal protection against any discrimination in violation of this Declaration and against any incitement to such discrimination.

Artcle 8. Everyone has the right to an effective remedy by the competent national tribunals for acts violating the fundamental rights granted him by the constitution or by law.

Article 9. No one shall be subjected to arbitrary arrest, detention or exile.

Article 10. Everyone is entitled in full equality to a fair and public hearing by an independent and impartial tribunal, in the determination of his rights and obligations and of any criminal charge against him.

Article 11. (1) Everyone charged with a penal offence has the right to be presumed innocent until proved guilty according to law in a public trial at which he has had all the guarantees necessary for his defence.

(2) No one shall be held guilty of any penal offence on account of any act or omission which did not constitute a penal offence, under national or international law, at the time when it was committed. Nor shall a heavier penalty be imposed than the one that was applicable at the time the penal offence was committed.

Article 12. No one shall be subjected to arbitrary interference with his privacy, family, home or correspondence, nor to attacks upon his honour and reputation. Everyone has the right to the protection of the law against such interference or attacks.

Article 13. (1) Everyone has the right to freedom of movement and residence within the borders of each state.

(2) Everyone has the right to leave any country, including his own, and to return to his country.

Article 14. (1) Everyone has the right to seek and to enjoy in other countries asylum from persecution.

(2) This right may not be invoked in the case of prosecutions genuinely arising from non-political crimes or from acts contrary to the purposes and principles of the United Nations.

Article 15. (1) Everyone has the right to a nationality.

(2) No one shall be arbitrarily deprived of his nationality nor denied the right to change his nationality.

Article 16. (1) Men and women of full age, without any limitation due to race, nationality or religion, have the right to marry and to found a family. They are entitled to equal rights as to marriage, during marriage and at its dissolution.

(2) Marriage shall be entered into only with the free and full consent of the intending spouses.

(3) The family is the natural and fundamental group unit of society and is entitled to protection by society and the State.

Article 17. (1) Everyone has the right to own property alone as well as in association with others.

(2) No one shall be arbitrarily deprived of his property.

Article 18. Everyone has the right to freedom of thought, conscience and religion; this right includes freedom to change his religion or belief, and freedom, either alone or in community with others and in public or private, to manifest his religion or belief in teaching, practice, worship and observance.

Article 19. Everyone has the right to freedom of opinion and expression; this right includes freedom to hold opinions without interference and to seek, receive and impart information and ideas through any media and regardless of frontiers.

Article 20. (1) Everyone has the right to freedom of peaceful assembly and association.

(2) No one may be compelled to belong to an association.

Article 21. (1) Everyone has the right to take part in the government of his country, directly or through freely chosen representatives.

(2) Everyone has the right of equal access to public service in his country.

(3) The will of the people shall be the basis of the authority of government; this will shall be expressed in periodic and genuine elections which shall be by universal and equal suffrage and shall be held by secret vote or by equivalent free voting procedures.

Article 22. Everyone, as a member of society, has the right to social security and is entitled to realisation, through national effort and international co-operation and in accordance with the organization and resources of each State, of the economic, social and cultural rights indispensable for his dignity and the free development of his personality.

Article 23. (1) Everyone has the right to work, to free choice of employment, to just and favorable conditions of work and to protection against unemployment.

(2) Everyone, without any discrimination, has the right to equal pay for equal work.

(3) Everyone who works has the right to just and favorable remuneration insuring for himself and his family an existence worthy of human dignity, and supplemented, if necessary, by other means of social protection.

(4) Everyone has the right to form and to join trade unions for the protection of his interests.

Article 24. Everyone has the right to rest and leisure, including reasonable limitation of working hours and periodic holidays with pay.

Article 25. (1) Everyone has the right to a standard of living adequate for the health and well-being of himself and of his family, including food, clothing, housing and medical care and necessary social services, and the right to security in the event of unemployment, sickness, disability, widowhood, old age or other lack of livelihood in circumstances beyond his control.

(2) Motherhood and childhood are entitled to special care and assistance. All children, whether born in or out of wedlock, shall enjoy the same social protection.

Article 26. (1) Everyone has the right to education. Education shall be free, at least in the elementary and fundamental stages. Elementary education shall be compulsory. Technical and professional education shall be made generally available and higher education shall be equally accessible to all on the basis of merit.

(2) Education shall be directed to the full development of the human personality and to the strengthening of respect for human rights and fundamental freedoms. It shall promote understanding, tolerance and friendship among all nations, racial or religious groups, and shall further the activities of the United Nations for the maintenance of peace.

(3) Parents have a prior right to choose the kind of education that shall be given to their children.

Article 27. (1) Everyone has the right freely to participate in the cultural life of the community, to enjoy the arts and to share in scientific advancement and its benefits.

(2) Everyone has the right to the protection of the moral and material interests resulting from any scientific, literary or artistic production of which he is the author.

Article 28. Everyone is entitled to a social and international order in which the rights and freedoms set forth in this Declaration can be fully realized.

Article 29. (1) Everyone has duties to the community in which alone the free and full development of his personality is possible.

(2) In the exercise of his rights and freedoms, everyone shall be subject only to such limitations as are determined by law solely for the purpose of securing due recognition and respect for the rights and freedoms of others and of meeting the just requirements of morality, public order and the general welfare in a democratic society.

(3) These rights and freedoms may in no case be exercised contrary to the purposes and principles of the United Nations.

Article 30. Nothing in this Declaration may be interpreted as implying for any State, group or person any right to engage in any activity or to perform any act aimed at the destruction of any of the rights and freedoms set forth herein.

SUGGESTED STUDY RESOURCES

UNITED NATIONS PUBLICATIONS:

These publications should be purchased from the nearest bookseller who stocks United Nations books. If in doubt as to his address, write to the Sales Section in New York. Should local stocks be exhausted at the time of your enquiry, please register the order with the bookseller, who will procure the titles requested as quickly as possible.

Bibliography of Current United Nations Publications on Human Rights

TEACHING HUMAN RIGHTS (United Nations, N.Y.)
A new edition of this 1959 handbook is currently in preparation and will be published by the United Nations in the autumn of 1963.

YEARBOOK ON HUMAN RIGHTS FOR 1959. 1962.
61.XIV.1. $5.00. Clothbound. 395 p.
Available in English. French edition in preparation.
(Previous editions of the YEARBOOK are also available).

THE UNIVERSAL DECLARATION OF HUMAN RIGHTS: A STANDARD OF ACHIEVEMENT
2nd edition, 1962.
62.I.9. $0.25. 38 p. Available in English.

UNITED NATIONS WORK FOR HUMAN RIGHTS. 1962.
62.I.3. $0.25. 40 p. Available in English and French.

FOR HUMAN WELFARE. 3rd edition, 1962.
62.I.20. $0.25. 52 p. Available in English.

LEGAL STATUS OF MARRIED WOMEN. Reprint, 1962.
57.IV.8. $0.75. 103 p. Available in English, French and Spanish.

CONVENTION ON THE POLITICAL RIGHTS OF WOMEN. HISTORY AND COMMENTARY. Reprint, 1962.
55.IV.17. $0.35. 46 p. Available in English and French.

THE UNITED NATIONS AND THE STATUS OF WOMEN. 1961.
61.I.9. $0.25. 28 p. Available in English.

STUDY OF DISCRIMINATION IN THE MATTER OF RELIGIOUS RIGHTS AND PRACTICES. 1961.
60.XIV.2. $1.00 79 p. Available in English, French and Spanish.

FREEDOM FROM ARBITRARY ARREST, DETENTION AND EXILE. (Yearbook on Human Rights: First Supplementary Volume). 1960.
59.XIV.2. $4.50. Clothbound. 249 p. Available in English and French.

THE UNIVERSAL DECLARATION OF HUMAN RIGHTS.
Leaflet.
$2.00 per hundred. Available in English, French and Spanish.

GENERAL ASSEMBLY OFFICIAL RECORDS.
16th Session. Third Committee. Social, Humanitarian and Cultural Questions. Summary records of meetings 1059-1134. 20 September-14 December 1961. 1962.
$4.50. 382 p. Available in English, French and Spanish.

GENERAL ASSEMBLY OFFICIAL RECORDS.
17th Session. Supplement No. 11. Report of the United Nations High Commissioner for Refugees, 1 April 1963-31 March 1962. (A/5211/Rev.1). 1962.
$0.50. 35 p. Available in English, French and Spanish.

GENERAL ASSEMBLY OFFICIAL RECORDS.
17th Session. Supplement No. 11A. Addendum to the Report of the United Nations High Commissioner for Refugees. (A/5211/Rev.1/Add.1). 1963.
$0.35. 14 p. Available in English, French and Spanish.

ECONOMIC AND SOCIAL COUNCIL OFFICIAL RECORDS.
34th Session. Supplement No. 7. Commission on the Status of Women. Report of the 16th Session, 19 March-6 April 1962. (E/3606/Rev.1;E/CN.6/403/Rev.1). 1962.
$0.50. 35 p. Available in English, French and Spanish.

ECONOMIC AND SOCIAL COUNCIL OFFICIAL RECORDS.
34th Session. Supplement No. 8. Commission on Human Rights. Report of the 18th session, 19 March-14 April 1962. (E/3616/Rev.1;E/CN.4/832/Rev.1). 1962.
$0.75. 46 p. Available in English, French and Spanish.

Copies of the previous sessions of the OFFICIAL RECORDS on human rights are also available.

UNITED NATIONS FILMSTRIPS

1. *The Universal Declaration of Human Rights*—Presents in graphic form the content and significance of the Universal Declaration of Human Rights. What these rights are, what they mean to all the world, is explained in terms of human beings. (73 frames with English captions or non-captioned versions with French, Spanish, English and Portuguese title frames; black and white drawings; suitable for secondary schools and adult groups).

2. *The International Trusteeship System*—The well-being and advancement of the people in Trust Territories and their progressive development toward self-government is a major concern of the United Nations. This filmstrip shows some of the progress of these dependent peoples toward these ends. (33 frames, with English, French or Spanish captions or non-captioned versions with English and Portuguese title frames; black and white photographs, suitable for junior groups, secondary schools and adult groups).

In the United States these filmstrips are available from Stanbow Productions, Inc., Valhalla, New York at $3.00 each; the latter filmstrip is available from the National Film Board of Canada, P.O. Box 6100, Montreal 3, Quebec, Canada. In other countries both filmstrips are available through the UN Information Centres.

UNESCO INFORMATION MATERIALS:

The following materials are available from the UNESCO Publications Center, 317 East 34th St., New York 16, N. Y.

Posters and Poster Sets

"The Gift of Knowledge," a photo feature on the UNESCO Gift Coupon Programme.   English, French.   Free.

"UNESCO and Human Rights," a set of 12 posters on the work of UNESCO in implementing the Universal Declaration, together with captions and discussion guide for classroom work. English, French, Spanish, Russian. $1.00.

"For all Children," a set of 10 posters on the Declaration of the Rights of the Child, together with captions and discussion guide for classroom use.   English, French, Russian. $1.00.

"Information for All," a photo feature of UNESCO's work promoting the freedom of information.   English, French, Spanish.   Free.

Brochures

Race and Culture—Michel Leiris, 44 p.	30¢
The Race Concept: Results of an Inquiry, 94 p.	85¢
Race Mixture—Harry L. Shapiro, 50 p.	50¢
The Significance of Racial Differences—G. Morant, 47 p.	30¢
Race and Society—Kenneth L. Little, 56 p.	30¢

Race and History—Claude Levy-Strauss, 40 p. .... 30¢
Racial Myths—Juan Comas, 49 p. .... 30¢
Race and Biology—L. C. Dunn, 46 p. .... 30¢
Race and Psychology—Otto Klineberg, 36 p. .... 30¢
The Roots of Prejudice—Arnold Rose, 34 p. .... 30¢
Race Relations and Mental Health—Marie Jahoda, 48 p. .... 50¢
The Jewish People—Harry L. Shapiro, 84 p. .... 70¢
The Race Question in Modern Science (series)
The Race Question in Modern Thought (series)
The Catholic Church and the Race Question—
   Rev. Fr. Yves M. J. Congar, O.P., 62 p. .... 50¢
The Ecumenical Movement and the Racial Problem—
   W. A. Visser'T Hooft, 70 p. .... 50¢
Jewish Thought as a Factor in Civilization—
   Prof. Leon Roth, 64 p. .... 50¢
Buddhism and the Race Question—G. P. Malalasekera and
   K. N. Jayatilleke, 74 p. .... 50¢
"*The Changing Social Position of Women in Japan,*" $2.00
"*The Education of Women for Citizenship,*" $1.50
"*The Emancipation of the Turkish Woman,*" $1.00
"*Flight and Resettlement,*" $3.50
"*The Political Role of Women,*" $2.50

Film Strips

(For terms write to UNESCO Publications Center)

"The Gift of Knowledge," 42 frames, colour, on the Unesco Gift
   Coupon Programme.
Human Rights Series, based on the UNESCO Exhibition on Human
   Rights, held in Paris in 1949. (Also available in Arabic and
   German).
"Milestones"—30 frames
"Abolition of Slavery"—30 frames
"Emancipation of Women"—30 frames
"Freedom of Thought"—30 frames
"Right to Education"—30 frames
"Arts and Life"—30 frames
"Rights of the Child," 40 frames, colour. Illustrates the Declaration
   of the Rights of the Child with the help of puppets.
"What is Race?" 32 frames, colour. Basic information about the bio-
   logical aspects of race, based on the Unesco booklet,
"What is Race?—Evidence from Scientists."

APPENDIX 3

THE GENERAL ASSEMBLY VOTES ON SOME KEY RESOLUTIONS

It should be noted that ALL the countries which voted on the resolutions referred to here, are NOT listed. For purposes of illustration, as explained below, only the voting records of countries with permanent membership on the Security Council and countries usually associated with the so-called Afro-Asian and Latin American 'blocs," are included.

The following General Assembly resolutions concern the United Nations peace-keeping operations of the United Nations Emergency Force (UNEF) in the Middle East, the Operations of the United Nations in the Congo (ONUC), the decision of the International Court of Justice on the status of expenditures for these two operations, the U.N. bond issue, and the decisions taken by the Assembly at the Fourth Special Session (1963) on the financial plight of the U.N. resulting from its costly peace-keeping operations. Many of the resolutions are the subject of deep dissension among Members, over the appropriate role of the United Nations in maintaining peace and security, or over the appropriate means to finance such peace-keeping operations.

The resolutions reviewed below have been selected because of their importance in establishing precedents for peace-keeping operations and their financing. Any future agreement for settling the out-standing problems mentioned above may well be based upon the precedents established in the past. For this reason, a knowledge of the past is imperative for an understanding of what may occur in the future.

Voting records of the Permanent Members of the Security Council, Members *usually associated with the so-called Afro-Asian and Latin American "blocs", are included to illustrate the areas of dissention and consensus among Members.* From this record, it is evident that there is no consistent pattern of voting among the Permanent Members of the Security Council, the Afro-Asians, and the Latin Americans. Each Member analyzes resolutions and the fundamental issues involved in light of its interests, and not in the interests of neighbors or of established powers.

On October 29, 1956, Israeli forces invaded Egypt and two days later, the United Kingdom and France intervened in the Suez Canal area. The resulting conflict was one of the most serious threats to peace and security since World War II, as it threatened to embroil in direct confrontation the major powers. The result would have been catastrophic both for the parties involved and all mankind. The United States immediately called a meeting of the Security Council. All resolutions put forward were vetoed. Under the Uniting for Peace Resolution the dispute was transferred to the General Assembly, called to order at its First Emergency Special Session for the specific purpose of considering the dispute. On November 2, the Assembly adopted its first resolution (Resolution 997) which called for a cease-fire, withdrawal of all forces, and the refrainment of all Members from introducing military goods into the troubled area. The vote on this resolution was as follows:

	For	*Against*	*Abstentions*
Permanent Members of Security Council	China USSR USA	France UK	
Afro-Asians	Afghanistan Burma Cambodia Ceylon Egypt Ethiopia India Indonesia Iran Iraq Jordan Lebanon Liberia Libya Nepal Pakistan Philippines Saudi Arabia Syria Thailand Yemen		Laos
Latin Americans	Argentina Bolivia Brazil Chile Colombia Costa Rica Cuba Dominican Republic Ecuador El Salvador Guatemala Haiti Honduras Mexico Nicaragua Panama Paraguay Peru Uruguay Venzuela		

On the same day that the above resolution was adopted, Canada suggested that a U.N. international force be constituted to supervise the cessation of hostilities. Consequently, in Resolution 998, the Assembly, on November 4, requested the Secretary-General to submit a plan for the establishment of an international emergency U.N. force to secure and supervise the cessation of hostilities in the Middle East area. Resolution 998 was adopted by a large majority.

	For	*Against*	*Abstentions*
Permanent Members of Security Council	China USA		France USSR UK
Afro-Asians	Afghanistan Burma Cambodia Ceylon Ethiopia India Indonesia Iran Iraq Jordan Lebanon Liberia Libya Nepal Pakistan Philippines Saudi Arabia Syria Thailand Yemen		Egypt Laos
Latin Americans	Argentina Bolivia Brazil Chile Colombia Costa Rica Cuba Dominican Republic Ecuador El Salvador Guatemala Haiti Honduras Mexico Nicaragua Panama Paraguay Peru Uruguay Venezuela		

Twelve hours after the General Assembly requested the Secretary-General to submit a plan on the emergency force, the Secretary-General submitted his first report. The Assembly, in Resolution 1000, noted with satisfaction the first report, established a United Nations Command for the proposed force, appointed its Commander, authorized the recruitment of officers for it, and invited the Secretary-General to take the necessary administrative steps for the full establishment of UNEF.

	For	*Against*	*Abstentions*
Permanent Members of Security Council	China USA		France USSR UK
Afro-Asians	Afghanistan Burma Cambodia Ceylon Ethiopia India Indonesia Iran Iraq Jordan Lebanon Liberia Libya Nepal Pakistan Philippines Saudi Arabia Syria Thailand Yemen		Egypt Laos
Latin Americans	Argentina Bolivia Brazil Chile Colombia Costa Rica Cuba Dominican Republic Ecuador El Salvador Guatemala Haiti Honduras Mexico Nicaragua Panama Paraguay Peru Uruguay Venezuela		

On November 6, 1956 the Secretary-General submitted a second report on UNEF. The next day, the General Assembly noted this report with appreciation, authorized the recruitment of personnel for UNEF, established an Advisory Committee to assist the Secretary-General in planning the force and its operations, and authorized the Secretary-General to issue all regulations and instructions to UNEF.

	For	*Against*	*Abstentions*
Permanent Members of Security Council	China France UK USA		USSR
Afro-Asians	Afghanistan Burma		Egypt
	Cambodia Ceylon Ethiopia India Indonesia Iran Iraq Jordan Laos Lebanon Liberia Libya Nepal Pakistan Philippines Saudi Arabia Syria Thailand Yemen		
Latin Americans	Argentina Bolivia Brazil Chile Colombia Costa Rica Cuba Dominican Republic Ecuador El Salvador Guatemala Haiti Honduras Mexico Nicaragua Panama Paraguay Peru Uruguay Venezuela		

On November 22, 1957, the General Assembly confirmed the principle established in a resolution of the previous year that the peace-keeping operations of the United Nations in the Middle East were the responsibility of all Members. The costs of UNEF for the rest of 1957 and 1958 were apportioned among all Members according to their scales of assessment for the regular budget. The vote on this resolution (1151) was as follows:

	For	Against	Abstentions
Permanent Members of Security Council	France UK USA	USSR	China
Afro-Asians	Afghanistan Burma Ceylon Ghana India Indonesia Iran Jordan Laos Liberia Pakistan Philippines Thailand		Cambodia Ethiopia Fed. of Malaya Iraq Lebanon Libya Morocco Nepal Saudi Arabia Sudan Syria Tunisia Yemen
Latin Americans	Argentina Bolivia Brazil Colombia Costa Rica Cuba Dominican Republic Haiti Honduras Nicaragua Paraguay Peru Uruguay Venezuela	Chile Ecuador	El Salvador Guatemala Mexico Panama

In 1959, the Assembly again apportioned the Middle East costs among Members according to their regular assessments, but at the same time, the Assembly recognized the hardships which the principal of collective responsibility placed upon those Members with the least capacity to share the responsibility in monetary terms. In Resolution 1441, the Assembly decided to use voluntary contributions to reduce by 50% the assessments of the poorest Members, beginning with those least capable of contributing to the expenses of UNEF. Such resolutions were to be made until the amount of voluntary contributions had been fully applied for this purpose.

	For	Against	Abstentions
Permanent Members of Security Council	France UK USA	USSR	China
Afro-Asians	Burma Cambodia Ceylon Fed. of Malaya Ghana India Indonesia Iran		Afghanistan Ethiopia Guinea Iraq Jordan Lebanon Libya Nepal

	Laos	Saudi Arabia
	Pakistan	Sudan
	Philippines	UAR
	Thailand	Yemen
	Tunisia	
Latin Americans	Argentina	Bolivia
	Brazil	Chile
	Colombia	Costa Rica
	Dominican Republic	Cuba
	Ecuador	El Salvador
	Haiti	Guatemala
	Honduras	Mexico
	Panama	Venezuela
	Paraguay	
	Peru	
	Uruguay	

On June 30, 1960, the Congo was granted independence by Belgium. The new state, however, was unable to keep law and order due to tribal wars and the mutiny of its army. The Congolese Government appealed for assistance from the United Nations, the United States and the Soviet Union. Because the Congo situation was ripe for the involvement of outside powers leading to another direct confrontation of the nuclear blocs, the United States Government told the Congolese to seek assistance from the United Nations. A series of Security Council meetings was called for this purpose in which several resolutions were passed establishing an international force to assist the Congolese Government in maintaining law and order and calling upon Belgium to withdraw its troops. The General Assembly then considered the problem at its Fourth Emergency Special Session in September, 1960. Assembly Resolution 1474 requested the Secretary-General to take vigorous action and to assist the Congo Government in restoring law and order throughout the country and in safe-guarding its territorial integrity and independence. The General Assembly also appealed to the Congolese for a speedy and peaceful solution to their problems, and called upon Members to refrain from providing arms to the Congolese factions except in conjunction with U.N. resolutions. To help defray the costs of ONUC, the Assembly appealed to Members for urgent voluntary contributions. The support of this resolution was as follows:

	For	*Against*	*Abstentions*
Permanent Mem-	China		France
bers of Security	UK		USSR
Council	USA		
Afro-Asians	Afghanistan		
	Burma		
	Cambodia		
	Ceylon		
	Ethiopia		
	Fed. of Malaya		
	Ghana		
	Guinea		
	India		
	Indonesia		

	Iran		
	Iraq		
	Jordan		
	Laos		
	Lebanon		
	Liberia		
	Libya		
	Morocco		
	Nepal		
	Nicaragua		
	Pakistan		
	Philippines		
	Saudi Arabia		
	Sudan		
	Thailand		
	Tunisia		
	UAR		
	Yemen		

Latin Americans — Argentina, Brazil, Chile, Colombia, Costa Rica, Cuba, Dominican Republic, Ecuador, El Salvador, Guatemala, Haiti, Honduras, Mexico, Nicaragua, Panama, Paraguay, Peru, Uruguay, Venezuela

In 1961, the General Assembly again considered the situation in the Congo. Resolution 1599 requested Belgium to accept its responsibilities as a member of the United Nations and to comply with the Security Council and the General Assembly resolutions. It also requested that all Belgian, other foreign military personnel, and mercenaries be withdrawn from the newly independent state.

	For	*Against*	*Abstentions*
Permanent Members of Security Council	China		France
	USSR		UK
			USA
Afro-Asians	Afghanistan	Nepal	Cameroun
	Burma		Central African
	Cambodia		Rep.

	Ceylon		Congo (L)
	Chad		Laos
	Congo (B)		Pakistan
	Dahomey		Philippines
	Ethiopia		Thailand
	Fed. of Malaya		

Gabon
Ghana
Guinea
India
Indonesia
Iran
Iraq
Ivory Coast
Jordan
Lebanon
Liberia
Libya
Madagascar
Mali
Morocco
Niger
Nigeria
Saudi Arabia
Senegal
Somalia
Sudan
Togo
Tunisia
UAR
Upper Volta
Yemen

Latin Americans	Cuba	Uruguay	Argentina
	Ecuador		Bolivia
	Nicaragua		Brazil
	Venezuela		Chile
			Colombia
			Costa Rica
			Dominican Rep.
			El Salvador
			Guatemala
			Haiti
			Honduras
			Mexico
			Panama
			Paraguay
			Peru

The General Assembly decided that the Congo operation expenses *for 1960* constituted "expenses of the Organization" within the meaning of Article 17, and as a result, the assessments against Members for ONUC were "binding legal obligations." Resolution 1583 further established an ad

103

hoc account for ONUC and apportioned the costs of the operation for 1960 among Members on the basis of the regular scale of assessments. Voluntary contributions were to be used to reduce by 50% the assessments of those Members least able to pay as was done for the financing of UNEF. A roll call vote was not taken on this resolution, but it was adopted by a vote of 46 to 17, with 24 abstentions.

In 1961, the General Assembly reverted back to the pattern used in financing UNEF. In Resolution 1619, the Assembly decided that the expenses for the Congo were essentially different in nature from the expenses of the Organization under the regular budget, and that the Permanent Members of the Security Council had a special responsibility for the maintenance of peace and security and the financing thereof. The Assembly also decided to apportion the costs of ONUC for 1961 among all Members in accordance with the regular scale of assessments for the regular budget, giving some relief to those states least capable of sharing the costs.

	For	*Against*	*Abstentions*
Permanent Members of Security Council	UK USA	USSR	China France
Afro-Asians	Burma Central African Republic Ceylon Chad Congo (L) Dahomey Ethiopia Fed. of Malaya Ghana India Iran Ivory Coast Laos Lebanon Liberia Libya Madagascar Nepal Nigeria Pakistan Philippines Senegal Somalia Thailand Togo Tunisia	Guinea Mali	Afghanistan Cambodia Gabon Indonesia Iraq Jordan Saudi Arabia Sudan UAR Upper Volta Yemen
Latin Americans	Columbia El Salvador Guatemala Nicaragua Panama	Brazil Cuba Mexico	Argentina Chile Bolivia Costa Rica Dominican Rep.

<pre>
                   Peru   Honduras
                   Uruguay   Venezuela
                   Paraguay   Ecuador
</pre>

General Assembly debate on all the preceding resolutions—and others—concerning the financing of UNEF and ONUC was embroiled in controversy over the legal nature of the expenses for the two peace-keeping operations. In all the resolutions, the Assembly recognized the responsibility of all Members for maintaining peace and security by apportioning the expenses of UNEF and ONUC among all Members according to their scale of assessments for the regular budget. Yet, in only one case concerning expenses for ONUC for 1960, did the General Assembly state that the expenses were "binding legal obligations." On December 20, 1961, the General Assembly decided to seek an advisory opinion from the International Court of Justice. They asked the Court whether or not expenditures by the United Nations for UNEF and ONUC constitute expenses within the meaning of Article 17, paragraph 2, of the Charter, and should therefore be borne by all members. The vote on whether to consult the court was:

	For	*Against*	*Abstentions*
Permanent Members of Security Council	UK USA	France USSR	China
Afro-Asians	Dahomey Fed. of Malaya Iran Ivory Coast Laos Liberia Libya Nigeria Pakistan Philippines Senegal Sierra Leone Thailand Tunisia Upper Volta		Afghanistan Burma Cameroun Central African Rep. Ceylon Chad Congo (L) Ethiopia Ghana Guinea India Indonesia Iraq Jordan Lebanon Madagascar Mali Mauritania Morocco Nepal Niger Somalia Sudan Syria Togo UAR Yemen
Latin Americans	Argentina Bolivia		Cuba

Brazil
Chile
Colombia
Costa Rica
Dominican Rep.
Ecuador
El Salvador
Guatemala
Nicaragua
Panama
Paraguay
Peru
Uruguay
Venezuela

The International Court of Justice, on 20 July 1962, submitted its opinion, ruling that United Nations expenses for UNEF and ONUC constituted expenses of the Organization within the meaning of the Charter. On December 19, 1962, the General Assembly adopted the Court's opinion. The vote was as follows:

	For	Against	Abstentions
Permanent Members of Security Council	UK USA China	France USSR	
Afro-Asians	Afghanistan Burma Burundi Cambodia Cameroun Central African Republic Ceylon Congo (B) Congo (L) Dahomey Ethiopia Fed. of Malaya Ghana India Indonesia Iran Laos Lebanon Liberia Libya Nepal Niger Nigeria Pakistan Philippines Rwandi Senegal	Jordan Madagascar Saudi Arabia Syria	Algeria Chad Iraq Sudan UAR

	Sierra Leone	
	Somalia	
	Tanganyika	
	Thailand	
	Togo	
	Tunisia	
Latin Americans	Argentina	Cuba
	Bolivia	
	Brazil	
	Chile	
	Colombia	
	Costa Rica	
	Dominican Rep.	
	Ecuador	
	El Salvador	
	Guatemala	
	Haiti	
	Honduras	
	Jamaica	
	Mexico	
	Nicaragua	
	Panama	
	Paraguay	
	Peru	
	Trinidad	
	Uruguay	
	Venezuela	

By December 1961, the United Nations was in a serious financial crisis caused by the costly expenditures for the two peace-keeping operations, and the refusal of some Members to contribute to the expenses of the operations and the tardiness of others in the payment of their assessments. The lack of funds endangered the ability of the United Nations to fulfill its responsibilities. As a result, the General Assembly resorted to an extraordinary measure to secure adequate financial resources until the Assembly could work out a long-range solution to the financial problem. On December 20, 1961, the General Assembly, in Resolution 1739, authorized the Secretary-General to issue United Nations bonds amounting to $200,000,-000, at 2% annual interest. The vote on Resolution 1739 was as follows:

	For	Against	Abstentions
Permanent Members of Security Council	UK	France	China
	USA	USSR	
Afro-Asians	Burma		Afghanistan
	Cameroun		Cambodia
	Ceylon		Central African
	Chad		Republic
	Ethiopia		Congo (L)
	Fed. of Malaya		India
	Ghana		Iraq
	Guinea		Jordan

107

	Indonesia		Libya
	Iran		Philippines
	Ivory Coast		Sudan
	Laos		**Syria**
	Lebanon		Togo
	Liberia		UAR
	Madagascar		Yemen
	Mali		
	Mauritania		
	Morocco		
	Nepal		
	Niger		
	Nigeria		
	Pakistan		
	Senegal		
	Sierra Leone		
	Somalia		
	Thailand		
	Tunisia		
	Upper Volta		

Latin Americans	Argentina	Cuba	Brazil
	Bolivia		Dominican
	Chile		Republic
	Colombia		Ecuador
	Guatemala		El Salvador
	Nicaragua		Haiti
	Panama		Mexico
	Paraguay		
	Peru		
	Venezuela		

The General Assembly met in Special Session from 14 May to 27 June 1963 to consider the financial problem facing the United Nations. Although a permanent solution to the problem was not reached, the Assembly did adopt a series of seven resolutions to ensure adequate financial resources through 1963. The first resolution adopted, Resolution 1874, established general principles to serve as guidelines for the sharing of costs of future peace-keeping operations involving heavy expenditures. Specifically, these principles are: (1) the financing of such operations is a collective responsibility of all Members, (2) while the economically more developed countries are in a position to make relatively larger contributions to the peace-keeping operations, the economically less developed countries have a relatively limited capacity to contribute, (3) every effort should be made to encourage voluntary contributions without prejudice to the principle of collective contributions, (4) the special responsibilities of the permanent members of the Security Council for the maintenance of peace and security should be borne in mind in connection with their contributions to the financing of peace and security operations, and (5) where circumstances warrant, the General Assembly should give special consideration to the situation of Members which are the victims of and those involved in events or actions leading to a peace-keeping operation. A roll call vote was not requested on Resolution 1874, but it was adopted by the Assembly by a vote of 92 to 11, with 3 abstentions.

108

In Resolution 1875, the second resolution adopted by the Special Session, the General Assembly appropriated $9.5 million for UNEF for the remainder of 1963; $2.5 million of this amount was to be assessed among all Members according to the regular scale of assessments. The remaining $7 million was to be based upon the regular scale of assessments except for the economically less developed countries who were to be billed at 45% of their rates under the regular scale. The vote on this resolution was as follows:

	For	Against	Abstentions
Permanent Members of Security Council	China UK USA	USSR	France
Afro-Asians	Afghanistan Burma Cambodia Cameroun Central African Republic Ceylon Chad Congo (B) Congo (L) Dahomey Ethiopia Fed. of Malaya Gabon Ghana India Indonesia Iran Ivory Coast Laos Lebanon Liberia Libya Madagascar Mauritania Nepal Niger Nigeria Pakistan Philippines Rwanda Senegal Sierra Leone Somalia Tanganyika Thailand Togo Tunisia Uganda Upper Volta		Algeria Burundi Guinea Iraq Jordan Kuwait Mali Saudi Arabia Sudan Syria UAR Yemen

Latin Americans	Argentina	Cuba	Peru
	Bolivia		
	Brazil		
	Chile		
	Colombia		
	Costa Rica		
	Dominican Republic		
	Ecuador		
	El Salvador		
	Guatemala		
	Honduras		
	Jamaica		
	Mexico		
	Nicaragua		
	Panama		
	Paraguay		
	Trinidad		
	Uruguay		
	Venezuela		

On the same day, the General Assembly, in Resolution 1876, authorized the Secretary-General to expend $33 million for ONUC through the remainder of 1963. Similar to the previous resolution, $3 million was to be apportioned to all Members according to their regular scale of assessments. The remaining $30 million was to be assessed to all Members according to the regular scale except for the economically less developed countries who were to be billed at 45% of their rates under the regular scale. The vote on this resolution was as follows:

	For	*Against*	*Abstentions*
Permanent Members of Security Council	China UK USA	USSR France	
Afro-Asians	Afghanistan		Algeria
	Burma		Chad
	Burundi		Iraq
	Cambodia		Jordan
	Cameroun		Kuwait
	Central African Republic		Madagascar Mali
	Ceylon		Saudi Arabia
	Congo (B)		Syria
	Congo (L)		UAR
	Dahomey		Yemen
	Ethiopia		
	Gabon		
	Ghana		
	Guinea		
	India		
	Indonesia		
	Iran		
	Ivory Coast		
	Laos		

110

Lebanon
Liberia
Libya
Malaya
Mauritania
Nepal
Niger
Nigeria
Pakistan
Philippines
Rwanda
Senegal
Sierra Leone
Somalia
Sudan
Tanganyika
Thailand
Togo
Tunisia
Uganda
Upper Volta

Latin Americans	Argentina	Cuba	Peru
	Bolivia		
	Brazil		
	Chile		
	Colombia		
	Costa Rica		
	Dominican Republic		
	Ecuador		
	El Salvador		
	Guatemala		
	Honduras		
	Jamaica		
	Mexico		
	Nicaragua		
	Panama		
	Paraguay		
	Trinidad		
	Uruguay		
	Venezuela		

APPENDIX 4

RANKING OF MEMBERS ACCORDING TO THE PERCENTAGE OF THEIR GNP CONTRIBUTED TO U.N.

1.	China	.489	45.	Cuba	.024
2.	Liberia	.248	46.	Italy	.024
3.	Congo (B)	.171	47.	Sudan	.024
4.	Libya	.153	48.	U.S.S.R.	
5.	Gabon	.115		(including Byelorussia &	
6.	Togo	.103		Ukraine)	.024
7.	Jordan	.084	49.	Argentina	.023
8.	Laos	.078	50.	Cameroon	.023
9.	Somalia	.071	51.	Ivory Coast	.022
10.	Netherlands	.070	52.	Yugoslavia	.022
11.	Norway	.069	53.	Albania	.021
12.	Sweden	.068	54.	Peru	.021
13.	Denmark	.067	55.	Burma	.021
14.	New Zealand	.054	56.	Spain	.021
15.	Iceland	.053	57.	Afghanistan	.020
16.	U.K.	.051	58.	Ecuador	.020
17.	Central African Rep.	.046	59.	Guatemala	.020
18.	Paraguay	.046	60.	Guinea	.020
19.	Canada	.044	61.	Iraq	.020
20.	Senegal	.044	62.	Ireland	.020
21.	Australia	.039	63.	Tunisia	.020
22.	U.S.A.	.038	64.	Venezuela	.020
23.	Iran	.036	65.	Chile	.019
24.	U.A.R.	.035	66.	South Africa	.019
25.	France	.035	67.	Chad	.018
26.	Bolivia	.034	68.	Niger	.018
27.	Belgium	.033	69.	Pakistan	.018
28.	Lebanon	.032	70.	Cambodia	.017
29.	Nicaragua	.031	71.	Mexico	.017
30.	Honduras	.031	72.	Ceylon	.017
31.	Haiti	.029	73.	Morocco	.017
32.	Costa Rica	.027	74.	Poland	.017
33.	Luxembourg	.027	75.	Colombia	.016
34.	Austria	.026	76.	Ghana	.016
35.	El Salvador	.026	77.	Dominican Republic	.016
36.	Czechoslovakia	.026	78.	Israel	.016
37.	India	.026	79.	Philippines	.016
38.	Uruguay	.026	80.	Portugal	.016
39.	Cyprus	.025	81.	Yemen	.016
40.	Thailand	.025	82.	Greece	.015
41.	Dahomey	.025	83.	Japan	.015
42.	Panama	.025	84.	Mali	.015
43.	Brazil	.024	86.	Nigeria	.015
44.	Finland	.024	87.	Ethiopia	.014

88. Tanganyika	.014	96. Turkey .009
89. Upper Volta	.014	97. Mongolia .008
90. Madagascar	.013	98. Bulgaria .007
91. Nepal	.013	99. Malaya .006
92. Saudi Arabia	.013	100. Mauretania .006
93. Hungary	.012	101. Congo (L) .005
94. Syria	.012	102. Indonesia .005
95. Rumania	.011	

(Contributions of Algeria, Burundi, Jamaica, Kuwait, Rwanda, Trinidad and Uganda were not yet determined by 1963).

APPENDIX 5
CONTRIBUTIONS PAYABLE BY MEMBER STATES TO THE UNITED NATIONS BUDGET FOR THE FINANCIAL YEAR 1963

Member States[a]	Scale of Assessments for 1963 %	Net Contributions for 1963 U.S. $
1. Afghanistan	0.05	39,459.00
2. Albania	0.04	31,965.00
3. Argentina	1.01	782,949.00
4. Australia	1.66	1,294,537.00
5. Austria	0.45	359,655.00
6. Belgium	1.20	941,070.00
7. Bolivia	0.04	30,126.00
8. Brazil	1.03	823,116.00
9. Bulgaria	0.20	159,930.00
10. Burma	0.07	55,911.00
11. Byelorussian Soviet Socialist Republic	0.52	415,674.00
12. Cambodia	0.04	31,965.00
13. Cameroun	0.04	31,965.00
14. Canada	3.12	2,451,553.00
15. Central African Republic	0.04	31,965.00
16. Ceylon	0.09	71,893.00
17. Chad	0.04	31,965.00
18. Chile	0.26	200,759.00
19. China	4.57	3,624,229.00
20. Colombia	0.26	207,637.00
21. Congo (Brazzaville)	0.04	31,965.00
22. Congo (Leopoldville)	0.07	56,018.00
23. Costa Rica	0.04	31,965.00
24. Cuba	0.22	169,817.00
25. Cyprus	0.04	31,965.00
26. Czechoslovakia	1.17	910,187.00
27. Dahomey	0.04	31,965.00
28. Denmark	0.58	451,230.00
29. Dominican Republic	0.05	39,231.00
30. Ecuador	0.06	47,733.00

31. El Salvador	0.04	31,255.00
32. Ethiopia	0.05	39,930.00
33. Federation of Malaya	0.13	103,778.00
34. Finland	0.37	295,699.00
35. France	5.94	4,667,518.00
36. Gabon	0.04	31,965.00
37. Ghana	0.09	71,973.00
38. Greece	0.23	177,048.00
39. Guatemala	0.05	39,518.00
40. Guinea	0.04	31,965.00
41. Haiti	0.04	30,801.00
42. Honduras	0.04	31,687.00
43. Hungary	0.56	447,877.00
44. Iceland	0.04	31,965.00
45. India	2.03	1,559,041.00
46. Indonesia	0.45	359,549.00
47. Iran	0.20	156,035.00
48. Iraq	0.09	70,165.00
49. Ireland	0.14	111,823.00
50. Israel	0.15	119,893.00
51. Italy	2.24	1,789,993.00
52. Ivory Coast	0.04	31,912.00
53. Japan	2.27	1,814,206.00
54. Jordan	0.04	31,965.00
55. Laos	0.04	31,965.00
56. Lebanon	0.05	39,956.00
57. Liberia	0.04	31,965.00
58. Libya	0.04	31,965.00
59. Luxembourg	0.05	38,658.00
60. Madagascar	0.04	31,912.00
61. Mali	0.04	31,965.00
62. Mexico	0.74	587,301.00
63. Morocco	0.14	111,876.00
64. Nepal	0.04	31,965.00
65. Netherlands	1.01	784,252.00
66. New Zealand	0.41	317,187.00
67. Nicaragua	0.04	31,810.00
68. Niger	0.04	31,965.00
69. Nigeria	0.21	167,814.00
70. Norway	0.45	349,562.00
71. Pakistan	0.42	335,682.00
72. Panama	0.04	30,586.00
73. Paraguay	0.04	31,965.00
74. Peru	0.10	77,673.00
75. Philippines	0.40	319,566.00
76. Poland	1.28	993,624.00
77. Portugal	0.16	127,752.00
78. Romania	0.32	255,664.00
79. Saudi Arabia	0.07	55,965.00
80. Senegal	0.05	39,930.00
81. Somalia	0.04	31,965.00

82. South Africa	0.53	403,749.00
83. Spain	0.86	687,054.00
84. Sudan	0.07	55,965.00
85. Sweden	1.30	1,015,280.00
86. Syria	0.05	39,947.00
87. Thailand	0.16	119,664.00
88. Togo	0.04	31,965.00
89. Tunisia	0.05	39,956.00
90. Turkey	0.40	313,292.00
91. Ukranian Soviet Socialist Republic	1.98	1,582,727.00
92. Union of Soviet Socialist Republics	14.97	11,951,498.00
93. United Arab Republic	0.25	195,532.00
94. United Kingdom of Great Britain and Northern Ireland	7.58	5,941,632.00
95. United States of America	32.02	28,582,212.00
96. Upper Volta	0.04	31,965.00
97. Uruguay	0.11	82,963.00
98. Venezuela	0.52	412,156.00
99. Yemen	0.04	31,965.00
100. Yugoslavia	0.38	285,465.00
	100.00	82,255,437.00
101. Mauritania	0.04	32,071.00
102. Mongolia	0.04	32,071.00
103. Sierra Leone	0.04	32,071.00
104. Tanganyika	0.04	32,071.00
	100.16	82,383,721.00

APPENDIX 6
DISCUSSION SUGGESTIONS
CHAPTER IX

(a) *Alleviating Frustrations*

    (1) Discuss the historical attempts by "have nots" to upset the status quo.

    (2) Compare the handicaps a poor nation faces with those a rich nation faces. What is a worse handicap, trained workers who die too young or high wages?

(b) *The U.N. as a School*

    (1) Discuss the impact of education on economic development. What historical examples can you study?

    (2) Discuss the implications of rivalries in giving aid. Does this distort the purpose of aid?

(3) What should be the purpose of aid?

(4) Discuss the need for compromise versus abiding by principles in a society.

(c) *Preventing Great Power Clashes*

(1) Discuss the possibility of a small conflict growing into a general war.

(b) *How well has the U.N. performed its four jobs?*

(1) Review the U.N. record. What crises have been settled with the help of the U.N.?

CHAPTER X

(1) Discuss the implications of abolishing the veto.

(2) Discuss the contradictions of those who both attack the veto and deplore the new majority of emergent nations in the U.N.

(3) Discuss world public opinion. Does it have an influence in the way public opinion has within a country? Why?

(b) *Majorities and Blocs*

(1) Discuss the alternatives given by Herbert Nicholas on pages 68-69: "either a U.N. sponsored policy, necessarily largely Afro-Asian manned, etc."

(2) Discuss the Herbert Nicholas arguments in the light of your earlier discussions on the veto.

CHAPTER XI

(a) *Picking up Messes*

    (1) Discuss alternatives to the U.N. operation in the Congo, why they were not adopted and their implications.

    (2) Discuss contention in the U.N. as a substitute for minor armed conflict. Does such verbal contention satisfy some of the urge to fight that nations harbour, according to psychologists.

    (3) Discuss the difference between dues that members pay to a private club and dues to the U.N.

CHAPTER XII

Discuss advantages of bilateral and multilateral aid.

STUDY GUIDE SERIES

Volume 1. **WORLD PEACE AND THE UNITED NATIONS**
- A World Safe To Live In
- The Rule of Law
- Refugees In Many Lands

Volume 2. **FOOD FOR LIFE — FOOD FOR THOUGHT**
- The World Must Eat (FAO and other agencies)*
- Building Peace in the Minds of Men (UNESCO)*

Volume 3. **TOWARD MANKIND'S BETTER HEALTH**
- Fighting Disease (WHO)*
- Toward A Better World For Children (UNICEF)*

Volume 4. **ENERGY AND SKILLS FOR HUMAN PROGRESS**
- The Human Needs of Labour (ILO)*
- Peaceful Uses of Atomic Energy (IAEA)

Volume 5. **FOR PEACE AND THE DIGNITY OF MAN**
- Human Rights*
- The United Nations — Who Needs It?*

Supplementary Volume **WORLD OF PROMISE**
- The United Nations Special Fund
- United Nations Technical Assistance
- The World Bank

*Also in separate booklets. Special quantity prices for schools and organizations on request.

Cloth volumes: 1-5, each $ 2.50   Paper volumes: 1-5, each $1.50

Set of 5 volumes: $12.50   Set of 5 volumes: $7.50

Supplementary volume: $ 3.50

7.